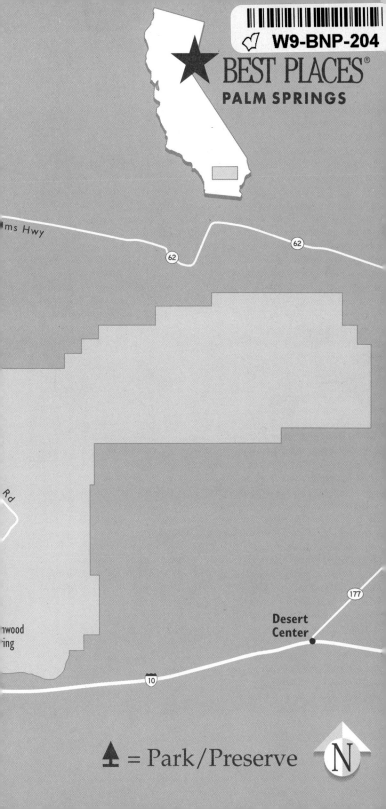

W9-BNP-204

BEST PLACES®
PALM SPRINGS

ms Hwy

62

62

Rd

177

**Desert
Center**

nwood
ing

10

🌲 = Park/Preserve

N

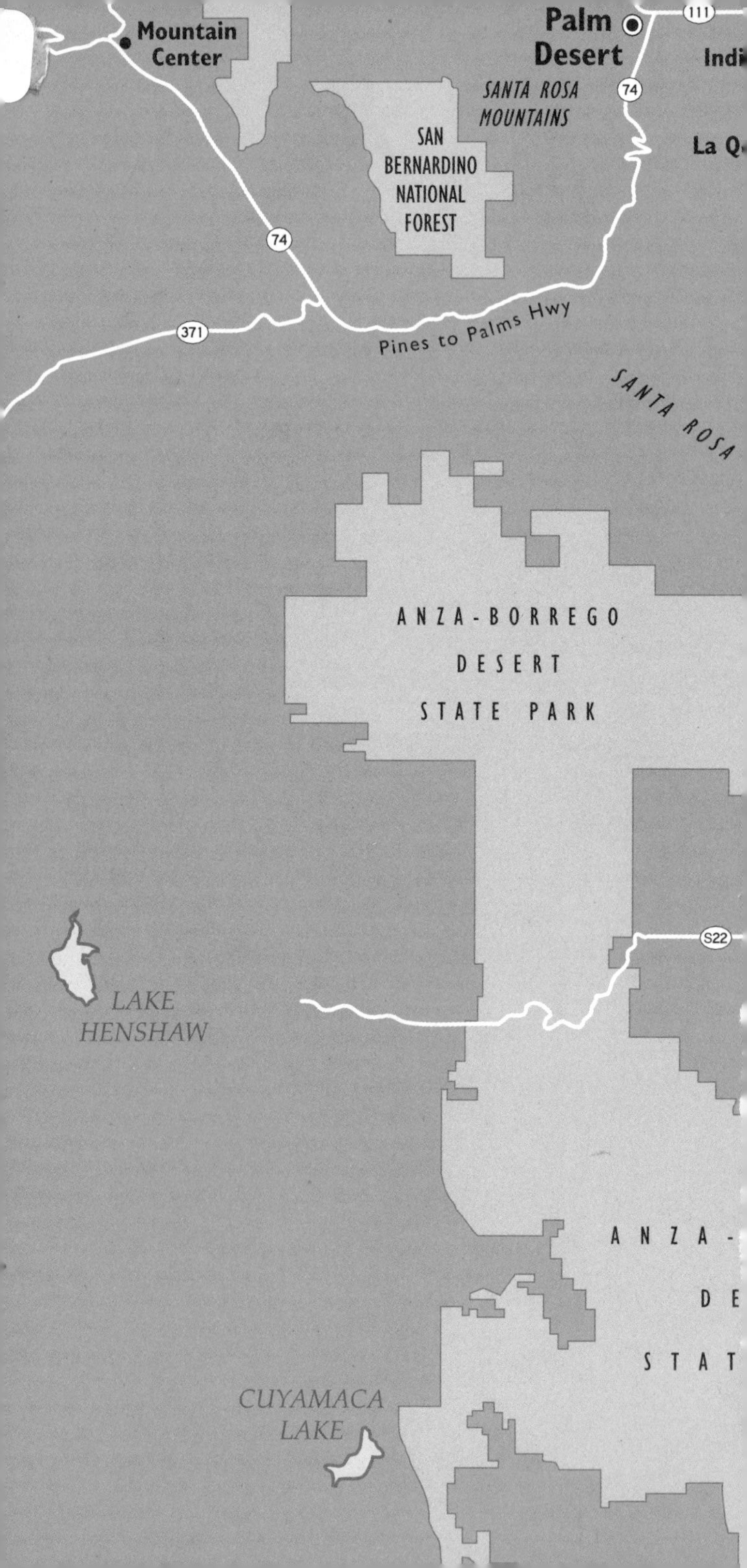

Mountain Center
Palm Desert
111
Indi
74
SANTA ROSA MOUNTAINS
La Q
SAN BERNARDINO NATIONAL FOREST
74
371
Pines to Palms Hwy
SANTA ROSA
ANZA-BORREGO DESERT STATE PARK
S22
LAKE HENSHAW
ANZA-
DE
STAT
CUYAMACA LAKE

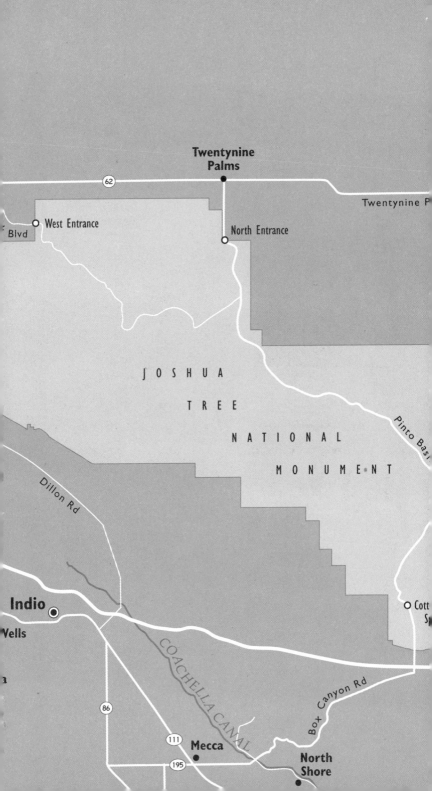

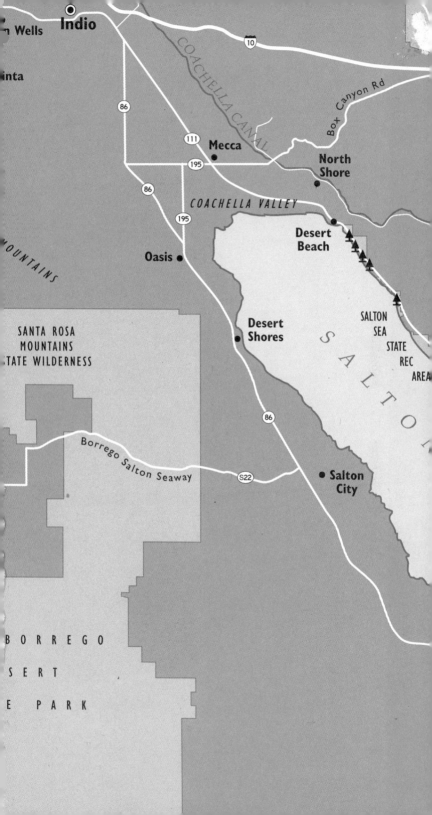

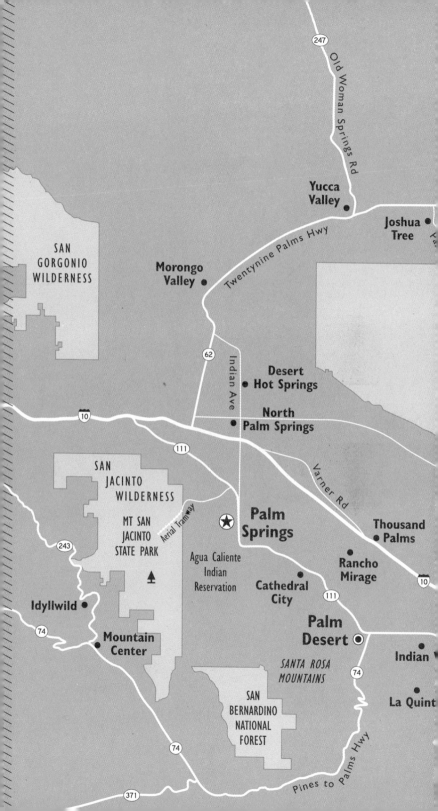

JOSHUA TREE
NATIONAL
MONUMENT

Desert
Center

10

BEST PLACES®
PALM SPRINGS

System Rd

COACHELLA CANAL

BOMBAY BEACH

111

SALTON SEA
NAT'L WILDLIFE
REFUGE

SEA

86

⚑ = Park / Preserve

N

Praise for Best Places® Guidebooks

"Best Places *covers must-see portions of the West Coast . . . with style and authority. In-the-know locals offer thorough info on restaurants, lodgings, and the sights.*"
—NATIONAL GEOGRAPHIC TRAVELER

"Best Places *are the best regional restaurant and guide books in America.*"
—THE SEATTLE TIMES

". . . *travelers swear by the recommendations in the* Best Places *guidebooks...*"
—SUNSET MAGAZINE

"*Known for their frank yet chatty tone . . .* "
—PUBLISHERS WEEKLY

"Best Places Southern California *is just about all the inspiration you need to start planning your next road trip or summer vacation with the kids.*"
—THE FRESNO BEE

"Best Places Southern California *and* Best Places San Diego *are quite good, and any traveler to the area would do well to pick one up.*"
—LIBRARY JOURNAL

"*Eat, surf, and shop like a local with this insider's guide,* Best Places San Diego.*"
—AMERICAN WAY

"Best Places San Francisco *has frank assessments of restaurants and accommodations . . .* "
—THE SEATTLE TIMES

"Best Places Northern California *is great fun to read even if you're not going anywhere.*"
—SAN FRANCISCO CHRONICLE

"*For travel collections covering the Northwest, the* Best Places *series takes precedence over all similar guides.*"
—BOOKLIST

"*The best guide to Seattle is the locally published* Best Places Seattle . . . "
—MONEY MAGAZINE

TRUST THE LOCALS

COMPLETELY INDEPENDENT
- No advertisers
- No sponsors
- No favors

EVERY PLACE STAR-RATED & RECOMMENDED

★★★★	The very best in the region
★★★	Distinguished; many outstanding features
★★	Excellent; some wonderful qualities
★	A good place
NO STARS	Worth knowing about, if nearby

PALM SPRINGS
AND THE DESERT COMMUNITIES

BEST PLACES®
DESTINATIONS

PALM SPRINGS
AND THE DESERT COMMUNITIES

IST EDITION
EDITED BY ROBIN KLEVEN

SASQUATCH BOOKS
SEATTLE

Printed in the United States of America.
Distributed in Canada by Raincoast Books, Ltd.
First edition
07 06 05 04 03 02 01   5 4 3 2 1

Series editor: Kate Rogers
Assistant editor: Laura Gronewold
Cover design: Nancy Gellos
Cover photo: ©Bob Rowan, Progressive Image/CORBIS
Foldout map: GreenEye Design
Interior design adaptation: Fay Bartels, Kate Basart, Millie Beard
Interior composition: Justine Matthies

ISSN: 1533-3965
ISBN: 1-57061-277-3

SASQUATCH BOOKS
615 Second Avenue
Seattle, WA 98104
(206)467-4300
books@SasquatchBooks.com
www.SasquatchBooks.com

Special Sales

BEST PLACES guidebooks are available at special discounts on bulk purchases for corporate, club, or organization sales promotions, premiums, and gifts. Special editions, including personalized covers, excerpts of existing guides, and corporate imprints, can be created in large quantities for specific needs. For more information, contact your local bookseller or Special Sales, Best Places Guidebooks, 615 Second Avenue, Suite 260, Seattle, Washington 98104, 800/775-0817.

CONTENTS

THE HIGH DESERT

IDYLLWILD

GOLF

ACKNOWLEDGMENTS

Working on my first book has been like unwrapping a series of gifts. As a native southern Californian, it's been an ongoing pleasure to revisit so many of my favorite places—and to discover hundreds of wonderful new treasures to share.

From Yucca Valley and Joshua Tree, through Palm Springs to Indio and Idyllwild, I've found a world of fascinating people who helped make this project a success. Many thanks to everyone who spoke with me in person, by phone, and via e-mail for the generous gift of their time and expertise.

I'm deeply grateful to my fellow Best Places editors and writers for their contributions from *Best Places Southern California*. Special thanks to Erika Lenkert and Peter Jensen, who provided beautifully written text and vital background information, and to outdoors writer (and former newsroom colleague) Ed Zieralski, who shared his extensive research on camping, hiking, and other fresh-air pursuits.

This book could not have been written without my fiancé, family, and friends, who provided constant support and encouragement. And finally, I'm forever grateful to the Sasquatch Books team of pros who guided me with through the entire process with style and grace, especially Laura Gronewold, Jennie McDonald, and Kate Rogers.

—*Robin Kleven*

ABOUT BEST PLACES GUIDEBOOKS

Palm Springs and the Desert Communities is part of the BEST PLACES guidebook series, which means it's written by and for locals, who enjoy getting out and exploring the region. When making our recommendations, we seek out establishments of good quality and good value, places that are independently owned, run by lively individuals, touched with local history, or sparked by fun and interesting decor. Every place listed is recommended.

BEST PLACES guidebooks, which have been published continuously since 1975, represent one of the most respected regional travel series in the country. Each guide is written completely independently: no advertisers, no sponsors, no favors. Our reviewers know their territory, work incognito, and seek out the very best a city or region has to offer. We provide tough, candid reports and describe the true strengths, foibles, and unique characteristics of each establishment listed.

Note: Readers are advised that the reviews in this edition are based on information available at press time and are subject to change. The editors welcome information conveyed by users of this book, as long as they have no financial connection with the establishment concerned. A report form is provided at the end of the book, and feedback is also welcome via email: books@SasquatchBooks.com.

HOW TO USE THIS BOOK

ACTIVITIES

Each town throughout this area has a variety of activities and attractions from which to choose. For quick and easy reference, we've created basic symbols to represent them, with full details immediately following. Watch for these symbols:

Architecture and historical sites

Arts and crafts, galleries

Beaches, swimming, water recreation

Bicycling

Bird-watching, other wildlife viewing

Boating

Celebrity-oriented activities

Entertainment: movies, theater, concerts, performing arts, events

Fishing

Food and drinks

Hikes and walks

Horseback riding

Kid-friendly, family activities

Local produce, farmers markets, street fairs

Museums and memorials

Parks, wilderness areas, outdoor recreation

Shops: clothing, books, antiques, souvenirs

Spas

Tennis

Views, scenic driving tours, attractions

RECOMMENDED RESTAURANTS AND LODGINGS

At the end of each town section you'll find restaurants and lodgings recommended by our BEST PLACES editors.

Rating System Establishments with stars have been rated on a scale of zero to four. Ratings are based on uniqueness, value, loyalty of local clientele, excellence of cooking, performance measured against goals, and professionalism of service.

(*no stars*)	Worth knowing about, if nearby
★	A good place
★★	Some wonderful qualities
★★★	Distinguished, many outstanding features
★★★★	The very best in the region

View Watch for this symbol throughout the book, indicating those restaurants and lodgings that feature a view.

Price Range Prices for lodgings are based on peak season rates for one night's lodging for two people (i.e., double occupancy). Off-season rates vary but can sometimes be significantly less. Prices for restaurants are based primarily on dinner for two, including dessert, tax, and tip. Call ahead to verify, as all prices are subject to change.

$$$$	Very expensive (more than $200 for one night's lodging for two)
$$$	Expensive (more than $100 for dinner for two; between $150 and $200 for one night's lodging for two)
$$	Moderate (between $40 and $100 for dinner for two; between $100 and $150 for one night's lodging for two)
$	Inexpensive (less than $40 for dinner for two; less than $100 for one night's lodging for two)

Email and Web Site Addresses We've included email and Web site addresses of establishments, where available. Please note that the World Wide Web is a fluid and evolving medium, and that Web pages are often "under construction" or, as with all time-sensitive information in a guidebook such as this, may be no longer valid.

Checks and Credit Cards Most establishments that accept checks also require a major credit card for identification. Credit cards are abbreviated in this book as follows: American Express (AE); Diners Club (DC); Discover (DIS); MasterCard (MC); Visa (V).

Directions Throughout the book, basic directions are provided with each restaurant and lodging. Call ahead, however, to confirm hours and location.

Bed-and-Breakfasts Many B&Bs have a two-night minimum-stay requirement during the peak season, and several do not welcome children. Ask about a B&B's policies before you make your reservation.

Smoking Most establishments in the Palm Springs area do not permit smoking inside, although some lodgings have rooms reserved for smokers. Call ahead to verify an establishment's smoking policy.

Pets Most establishments do not allow pets; call ahead to verify, however, as some budget places do.

Index All restaurants, lodgings, town names, and major tourist attractions are listed alphabetically at the back of the book.

Reader Reports At the end of the book is a report form. We receive hundreds of reports from readers suggesting new places or agreeing or disagreeing with our assessments. They greatly help in our evaluations. We encourage you to respond.

THE LOW DESERT

THE LOW DESERT

With its searing temperatures, soaring mountains, and a land-locked sea almost 230 feet below sea level, the low desert, which encompasses the Coachella Valley and Salton Basin, remains a place of baffling, exciting incongruities. On one hand, humans have made every effort to turn much of the long, level valley's sand and rock into a vast necklace of emerald-green golf courses surrounded by resorts, malls, and new residential colonies. Despite this, nature continues to hold the winning hand here and to do what she pleases. Flash floods roar off the mountain flanks and tumble through washes that otherwise might stay bone-dry for years. Dead-calm mornings turn into afternoons riven by moaning winds, often powerful enough to knock a bejeweled Palm Desert matron right out of her stiletto heels.

In geologic nomenclature, the entire area is called the Salton Basin, the Salton Trough, or sometimes the Salton Sink. It stretches from San Gorgonio Pass near Palm Springs to the Salton Sea and beyond, fanning out over the U.S.–Mexico border and eventually disappearing into the Gulf of California. Although these low-down names may sound clumsy, they aptly describe an entire region that was lowered (in some places to as much as 230 feet below sea level) over millions of years by earth movement along the San Andreas fault. Simultaneously, the San Andreas helped lift the Sink's adjacent mountains to 10,000 feet or more. Snowcapped in winter, these ranges, the San Jacinto and San Gorgonio, tower over the region like a chain of Alps on Mars.

Jumbled and hostile, they rise along the south side of Highway 111 in Palm Springs, Rancho Mirage, Palm Desert, and Indian Wells. Once you climb above about 5,000 feet, the summits soften under a cloak of pine and fir trees. Palm Springs's famed tramway whisks you from the valley floor into this forest, where the air is far cooler and the desert seems a continent away rather than a few miles below. Even with this cool escape, and enough air-conditioning in every car and building to frost your earlobes, the valley clears out from June through September, as 110°F-plus temperatures become breathtakingly common.

Naturally, the desert's heat is also why everyone loves the Big Sink, especially in "the Season" (winter and spring), when days stay in the '70s but nights are chilly enough for you to light a fire

What's the weather like today in the desert? Log onto www.desert-resorts.com to find the current temperature and forecast for the next day.

LOW DESERT THREE-DAY TOUR

DAY ONE: *Spend the morning browsing the shops and galleries along S Palm Canyon Drive in downtown Palm Springs. Don't miss the* **Village Green Heritage Center,** *where you'll get a sense of the city's early history. Duck in for lunch at* **Las Casuelas Terraza,** *then drive a few blocks into the old Tennis District to check into your room at* **Korakia Pensione.** *After a swim and a nap, drive 6 miles northwest of Palm Springs to catch the* **Palm Springs Aerial Tramway,** *on which you'll ascend almost 6,000 feet up the mountainside to Mountain Station. Stay long enough to enjoy the view and have a light snack on the aerielike terrace. Return to your room for a freshen-up, then walk to dinner at nearby* **St. James at the Vineyard.**

DAY TWO: *Rise early, take your time with coffee and continental breakfast in Korakia's courtyard, then drive about a half hour "down valley" on Highway 111 to Palm Desert. Breakfast fans might want to stop at* **Keedy's Fountain & Grill** *for huevos rancheros. Next, learn which plants and critters call the desert home with a visit in the cool of midmorning to nearby* **Living**

in your resort cottage's living room. Golf is nearly perfect here in winter, and almost a hundred courses now dot the landscape. Tennis, too: you can hear the racquet-on-ball thwacks emanating from every hotel and country-club grounds. Swimming pools, considered by tourists and residents alike to be an essential element of existence, host the bronzed, the bored, and the beautiful.

No trip to the low desert can be complete without a taste of all worlds, from the wilderness of a hidden palm canyon to the glitzy shopping gulch known as El Paseo in the city of Palm Desert. Visitors can golf in the morning, take a jeep trek in the afternoon, and then savor fine French cuisine by candlelight in an open courtyard in the evening. Nothing is too improbable. As one local hotel manager aptly put it, "Palm Springs is a small town—with everything you want."

In fact, the entire Coachella Valley maintains a small-town feeling. It takes under an hour to drive from Palm Springs at the west end to Indio in the east—half that to get from Palm Springs to Palm Desert.

Desert. Backtrack to downtown Palm Desert for a big salad and a smoothie at casual and lively Native Foods. Spend a few hours poking into all the elegant shops and galleries along El Paseo. Head north from Palm Desert to the Coachella Valley Preserve, which is open until sunset. Venture out in the evening on foot for drinks and dinner at Kaiser Grille, followed by a live performance at either the Annenberg Theater in the Palm Springs Desert Museum or the historic Plaza Theatre.

DAY THREE: Spend the morning playing golf on one of the Coachella Valley's nearly 100 golf courses, then return to your lodgings for one last swim, and check out. If you've worked up an appetite, try the Elvis Burger at the Burger Factory in Palm Springs, then stroll through the spiny world of Moorten Botanical Gardens. You'll also have time in the afternoon for a visit to Palm Springs Desert Museum, where art and natural history cohabitate in a splendid building against the mountainside. If a special milestone (especially a romantic one) needs celebrating, wind up the day with a champagne toast at Le Vallauris, followed by a candlelit dinner on their patio.

The valley first gained fame in the early 1900s as a sanitarium for wheezing asthmatics and tuberculosis victims who made their way here on doctors' orders to breathe the clean, dry air. The Hollywood set arrived in the 1920s and never really left. Frank Sinatra, Dean Martin, and Sammy Davis Jr. enlivened the 1950s and 1960s. Busts followed booms, but through it all the mountains watched in purple majesty. And the air—well, the air here, warm and dry as sable, just feels so very, very good.

ACCESS AND INFORMATION

Palm Springs International Airport (3400 E Tahquitz Canyon Wy; 760/323-8161) is served from major cities around the United States by Alaska, American, American Eagle, United, America West Express, United Express, and U.S. Airways Express. However, many airlines offer far less frequent service during the hot "out of season" months, June through September. Car rentals (Avis, Budget, Dollar, Hertz, National) are available in Palm Springs at the airport or directly through the valley resorts.

Most travelers touring the low desert approach via car on Interstate 10 from the Riverside/San Bernardino area. The final changeover of coastal plain to inland desert occurs as you travel through San Gorgonio Pass (famed for its weird forests of giant electricity-generating windmills). Immediately after the pass, with Mount San Gorgonio (elevation 11,499) to the north and Mount San Jacinto (elevation 10,804) to the south, Highway 111 splits off southward from the interstate, enters typical desert scenery of sand, rock, and scrub, and soon becomes a multilane boulevard (with traffic lights) that strings along from one desert resort community to the next—Palm Springs, Cathedral City, Rancho Mirage, Palm Desert, Indian Wells, and Indio. At Indio, a traveler can continue south to see the immense Salton Sea and its bird life, or rejoin Interstate 10 via Auto Center Drive. Interstate 10 continues east to enter Arizona at Blythe and is the primary route to Phoenix.

The Salton Sea area is close to Anza-Borrego Desert State Park, and travelers can make a giant loop tour of Southern California's deserts by going west from Salton Sea on Highway S22 into Anza-Borrego, south briefly to Highway 78, west to Highway 79, north to Aguanga and Highway 371, and east to Highway 74, which descends back into Palm Desert. Another route "over the hill" (and out of the desert) is State Route 74, also known as the Pines-to-Palms Highway. Route 74 enters the San Bernardino National Forest and leads to the mountain town of Idyllwild. It also facilitates a return to Los Angeles or San Diego via Interstate 15.

Keep abreast of the area's highway conditions by calling the California Highway Patrol's toll-free hotline, 800/427-7623. High winds often kick up sand in open areas outside of cities, causing poor visibility, dangerous conditions for big rigs and recreational vehicles, and, at the very least, damaged auto finishes. The hotline is also handy for finding out about road closures, detours, and delays.

PALM SPRINGS

In a letter to a friend in 1914, the widow of famed author Robert Louis Stevenson wrote, "There is . . . a climate of extraordinary purity and dryness, and almost no rain or wind. Wonderful cures . . . have taken place here. . . . if I had only known of Palm Springs in my Louis's time!" In those early days, weak-lunged patients gathered in tents amidst the palm groves, and there was no notion that the city of today—a place of glamour, golf, and dozens of restaurants, all grilling New York steaks and pouring big healthy shots of Johnnie Walker Red Label—might ever exist.

The first big boom hit in the 1920s. Bungalow courts and small motels sprang up, along with a few larger resorts. The Hollywood crowd swept in to vacation in the glorious, dry winter heat, arriving in automobiles that could negotiate the improving road system linking L.A. to this formerly remote location. Some of these old lodgings remain, as do others from subsequent booms in the 1950s and 1960s, when Frank Sinatra, Bob Hope, President Eisenhower, Liz Taylor, and a host of other big names kept P.S. in the limelight. But by the 1980s Palm Springs was dying, and its reputation had taken a serious drubbing from wild Spring Break weeks, when thousands of students arrived to party. Most of the fine stores abandoned downtown (Palm Desert became the new mecca for shopping and galleries), leaving it to the T-shirt and curio shops.

The story doesn't stop there, however. In 1988, the late entertainer and Palm Springs resident Sonny Bono ran for mayor—and won. Along with promoting the city as a family-friendly destination and increasing the enforcement of drinking laws, Bono created his notorious ban on thong bikinis. (Indeed, you'll still see signs at the occasional hotel pool reading "No thongs allowed.") Spring Break mellowed considerably, the collegiate crowd headed for greener—or barer—pastures, the locals were pleased, and Bono later went on to become a congressman.

Since then, Palm Springs has undergone a renaissance. *Vanity Fair* magazine called it "hot, hot, hot!" in their June 1999 issue. *Condé Nast Traveler* sees Palm Springs as "the new home of hip," while the distinguished *New Yorker* magazine praised the city's "nostalgia for a lifestyle of cocktails, cigars, Sinatra, and poolside cha-cha-cha."

The celebrities are back, visiting at exclusive resorts like the La Mancha Villas or buying sprawling homes in the hills. Hipsters have discovered Palm Springs as an enclave of 1950s architecture, much of it by internationally acclaimed Southern California design masters like Richard Neutra and R. M. Schindler.

If you buy a cactus or succulent to take home, don't forget to water it now and then. Moorten's Botanical Garden recommends giving these plants a drink once every week or two, when the soil dries out.

The area is also home to a thriving, highly visible gay crowd, many of whom stay at hotels and resorts catering exclusively to gay men and women. European guests are flocking to the valley in droves—often, during the scorching summer season when prime accommodations go for bargain basement prices. And the seasonal "snowbirds" from the northern U.S. and Canada never stopped coming to nest here during the winter months.

As you tour Palm Springs and the surrounding region's major attractions and other communities, keep the notion of "down-valley" in mind: Residents think of Palm Springs as being at the head of the Coachella Valley, and other desert communities to the southeast are all down-valley from here.

The gallery, shopping, and restaurant scene along S Palm Canyon Drive, which runs one-way, north-south between Amado Road and Ramon Road, saw a dramatic turnaround in the late 1990s. Shopping developments on Palm Canyon Drive include the Desert Fashion Plaza, anchored by a Saks Fifth Avenue, and the upscale Vineyard (corner of Baristo Road and Palm Springs Promenade). But don't overlook the dozens of charming and fascinating individual shops that line Palm Springs's main streets. Within one block, the merchandise can vary from estate jewelry and antiques to '50s memorabilia, original paintings, beauty supplies, tacky souvenirs, and designer clothing.

If you're trying to go north in the downtown area, by the way, you'll need to get on Indian Canyon Drive, just a block east of Palm Canyon Drive. It, too, is a one-way thoroughfare for part of its length, something to remember if you're driving in the city for the first time.

Toward the mountains, the Heritage District (called by locals "the tennis club district") features a concentration of small hotels, inns, and bed-and-breakfasts, many of them with a retro feeling. Visitors staying in this neighborhood can walk to Palm Canyon Drive, or stroll in the other direction toward the mountains and pick up a hiking trail that rambles over the wild desert mountainside.

For an overview of Palm Springs area events and activities, contact the Visitors Information Center (2781 N Palm Canyon Dr, at the north edge of the city, just south of the turnoff to the aerial tramway; 760/778-8418 or 800/347-7746; www.palm-springs.org). You can pick up a free, comprehensive Visitors

Guide at the center, or order one by phone or through the Web site. In addition to the standard city guides, they also have a special guide for the mobility-impaired traveler and a Visitors Guide especially for gay men and women. Need a hotel reservation? The center can do that too, for free—checking rates and availability before booking your room, and providing you with a confirmation number.

ACTIVITIES

Take the tram. The Palm Springs Aerial Tramway (760/325-1391; www.pstramway.com), a favorite attraction for close to 40 years, has undergone a dramatic and impressive renovation. Originally opened in 1963, the tram that rises from the desert floor to the mile-high forest has always been a must-visit for tourists, as well as a popular day trip for locals. After closing for more than three months, the tram reopened in September 2000 with new, state-of-the-art cars that hold 80 passengers and cost almost a half a million dollars each. The two tramcars, imported from Switzerland, are fitted with floors that rotate 360 degrees as the cars ascend into Mount San Jacinto State Park.

To reach the starting point, at the north end of Palm Springs, take Tramway Road off Highway 111 for 3.5 miles to Valley Station. Here, you'll get tickets for the dramatic ride, which takes about 15 minutes to climb 5,800 feet into the park. Along the way, watch the landscape change from one ecosystem to the next, as the transformation from low desert to mountain ridge progresses.

Up top at Mountain Station, it's quite literally a different world. At 8,500 feet, it's always much cooler than in the valley, so bring a sweater in June and a parka in January. You can stay for a couple of hours or a couple of days; primitive campsites are located within 2.6 to 7 miles from the upper tram station. Camping requires a permit, so be sure to obtain one in advance from Mt. San Jacinto State Wilderness (PO Box 308, Idyllwild, CA 92349; 909/659-2607). And of course, you'll need to bring your own equipment.

Most visitors come up for a few hours of hiking and quiet contemplation, but Mountain Station also has the requisite gift shop,

No matter which canyons you visit, be sure to bring plenty of drinking water if you plan to hike. The streams, while clear and inviting, aren't a source of potable water. And watch your step, especially during the spring. Rattlesnakes thrive in these parts, and while they won't go out of their way to bite, they will bite if threatened, stepped on, or touched. Finally, remember the usual desert combo: sunscreen and a hat.

snack bar, and cocktail lounge. During the summer, an old-fashioned mule train offers rides on sure-footed mounts.

The park features 54 miles of hiking and backpacking trails in summer, many of which become prime cross-country skiing and snowshoeing trails in winter when snow blankets the area. You can rent equipment at the tram station's Nordic Ski Center (760/327-6002) from the first snow of the winter through early April. Activities include snowshoeing, inner tubing, and cross-country skiing.

Tram cars depart at least every half hour from 10am Monday through Friday; from 8am weekends. Last car up leaves at 8pm with the last car down at 9:45pm. The schedule can vary, so call in advance if you need exact departure and arrival information. Year-round, a ride-and-dine package includes a sunset dinner at the tram's mountaintop restaurant (average food but incredible views of the valley) followed by a spectacular descent beneath a night sky so dark and clear the Milky Way really does look like spilled milk. The cost for a tram ride only is $20 for adults, $12.50 for kids. Annual passes are $110 for adults, $80 for kids 3 to 12.

Indian Canyons. Ask longtime residents where they go to hike, impress out-of-towners, or simply commune for a while with nature, and a majority will cite the nearby Indian Canyons (760/325-3400 or 800/790-3398; www.indiancanyons.com).

Owned by the Agua Caliente band of Cahuilla Indians, these canyons are spectacularly beautiful as well as culturally and historically fascinating. Three of the canyons—Andreas, Murray, and Palm—have been open to the public for many years, while a fourth, Tahquitz, has recently been reopened to visitors. The canyons serve as wildlife refuges as well as home to Washingtonia palms—the hardy survivors from 10,000-plus years ago, when the climate here was much wetter. And centuries ago, the canyons supported the local Cahuilla Indians, who used the mountain-fed streams to irrigate crops and built communities within the canyons themselves.

Visit the three canyons by heading four miles south of Palm Springs on S Palm Canyon Drive (Highway 111), following the signs that say Indian Canyons, to the reservation entrance, where you'll pay an admission fee and receive a map. Then follow the

THOSE WONDERFUL "MOP TOPS"

Stand on the floor of the Coachella Valley with your feet planted on a sidewalk in Palm Springs. Look south toward the San Jacinto Mountains. Forbidding, no? A massive pile of crushed rock, barely able to sustain life? True, and not so true, for no plant symbolizes the opportune nature of desert flora more than the noble native fan palm (Washingtonia filifera) found in the many folded canyons of the San Jacinto and Santa Rosa Mountains. Here in the palm groves, usually hidden from view to everyone but hikers, the hardy trees send down their thirsty roots toward year-round subterranean springs.

In winter these same canyons come to life with roaring freshets. And out on the desert floor, a few oases such as Thousand Palms also sustain these rustling 50-foot-tall trees. As you walk among them, look closely for the many inhabitants of and visitors to these wildlife "condominiums"—especially tree frogs and birds such as hooded orioles. Some palms wear "skirts" of dead fronds down much of their trunk length. If a palm is naked, it was probably the victim of sparks from a campfire or vandalism.

The best place to view these palm groves is one of the Indian Canyons. After you pass the entry station, continue on to Andreas Canyon, where you can park and hike less than a mile into Murray Canyon. For a longer hike, visit Palm Canyon, where about 3,000 palms line a 7-mile stretch of canyon.

signs to the various canyons, each of which offers marked hiking trails in varying degrees of difficulty. One of the most popular hikes is the half mile up through the Andreas Canyon; it's not too difficult, and towering rock formations, a gurgling year-round stream, varied plant life, and skittering lizards make for a delightful walk. Longer and more difficult trails originate from Murray Canyon, the least-visited of the three areas, and the Trading Post at Palm Canyon, about 2.5 miles from the entrance. (Don't attempt the road to the Trading Post in an RV; tight turns and rock formations make it impossible.)

Once at the post, you'll find a shaded picnic area and a small store that sells maps, books, refreshments, Indian music, pottery, and much more. One especially useful map is "Palm Canyon

A tiny band of wild horses lives in the hills above Palm Canyon and can sometimes be seen along the West Fork Trail. Rangers caution horseback riders to keep their distance; these native ponies can be territorial.

Indian Trails," which has detailed descriptions of more than a dozen hiking routes and a contour map with all trails and elevations clearly marked. Tribal rangers offer regularly scheduled guided hikes at each of the canyons—a terrific way to learn about Indian culture and local geology, wildlife, and ecology. The canyons are open daily for hiking and horseback riding—no camping, overnight stays, mountain biking, off-roading, or rock climbing allowed. A favorite destination of locals and tourists (including tour buses) during winter and spring, this is a place you can pretty much have to yourself on a midweek summer day when the temperature reaches three digits. General admission is $6 for adults, with discounts for seniors and kids; the equestrian fee is $7.

Big news surrounds the fourth canyon, Tahquitz, which had been closed since the late 1960s due to damage by visitors who vandalized the rock paintings and left mountains of trash. After an extensive trail-building and cleanup effort, this canyon is being opened to the public again. Rocky Toyama, director of the reservation's Tribal Rangers, says that Tahquitz Canyon has one of the most beautiful waterfalls in the desert (parts of the 1937 movie *Lost Horizon* were filmed here); you'll also find old irrigation systems and food preparation areas of the Native Americans, as well as other artifacts dating back thousands of years. As in the other canyons, hiking is permitted, but mountain biking and rock climbing, which could disturb this fragile ecological system, are not. For access and information, drop by the new visitors center at the end of Mesquite Street (take S Palm Canyon Dr 1 block east of the Rock Garden Café, 777 S Palm Canyon Dr, and turn toward the mountains). It's open every day 7:30am to 5pm; admission is $10 for adults, $5 for children. (Toyama hopes the canyon will remain open year round.) For updated information, call 760/325-3400.

 Agua Caliente Cultural Museum. Get a closer look at the native Cahuilla Indian culture at this museum (219 S Palm Canyon Dr; 760/323-0151; www.aguacaliente.org) devoted to historical and cultural artifacts. Photos, a botanical garden, dioramas, and exhibits help to tell the story of the people and how they lived. Hours are usually Wed to Sun, with limited hours during summer. Call ahead for specific times of operation. Free.

Botany 101. The well-tended Moorten Botanical Gardens offer a quick tour of deserts around the globe in the

span of a half hour's walk. Rather than brilliant flowers and lush greenery, this otherworldly acreage boasts 3,000 varieties of hardy desert plants. Founded by Patricia Moorten, a botanist, and her late husband, the collection features a stunning variety of local flora as well as imports collected by the Moortens on trips abroad.

Take the self-guided walking tour, and you'll pass succulents, smoke trees, agaves, and ocotillos; spiky plants, fuzzy plants, fragrant plants, alien-looking plants. Don't miss the greenhouse-like "cactarium," where hundreds of rare, weird, and wonderful cacti flourish, some of them reaching out to snag clothing à la Audrey in *Little Shop of Horrors*. Kids should enjoy the iguanas, doves, and desert tortoises on display, as well as the plant oddities; just make sure those little fingers and toes stay away from the spines. The grounds are available for weddings, receptions, and other celebrations; call for rates and availability. Ready to start your own cactarium? A variety of plants, both common and rare, are offered for sale at reasonable prices (1701 S Palm Canyon Dr; 760/327-6555; open daily except Wed; $2 for adults, 95 cents for kids).

Magnificent museum. From desert creatures to Diebenkorn: That sums up the eclectic, something-for-everyone approach at the big-city-sophisticated Palm Springs Desert Museum (101 Museum Dr; 760/325-0189 or 760/325-7186; www.psmuseum.org). Nestled in a deep well of landscaped sculpture gardens set up against the mountainside, the museum showcases paintings, sculpture, and Native American artifacts as well as the natural sciences. The permanent collection spans the spectrum from classic Western scenes and memorabilia to modern masterworks by Andy Warhol, George Segal, and Richard Diebenkorn. Kids and others with a fondness for creepy-crawlies can check out Desert Night and Day (in the McCallum Natural Science Wing), home to live desert denizens like hairy scorpions, snakes, and assorted rodents. (Open Tues–Sat, 10am–5pm, Sun noon–5pm; closed Mon and major holidays; $7.50 for adults, $6.50 for seniors 62 and over, $3.50 for youths 6–17, students, and active military personnel with I.D; free to kids under 6; free public admission the first Fri of each month, except during special exhibitions. From N Palm Canyon Dr heading south, turn

SCENIC NEIGHBORHOOD

One especially lovely section of Palm Springs is the neighborhood just west of the Palm Springs Desert Museum, bordered roughly by Tahquitz Canyon Way, Palm Canyon Drive, and Vista Chino Drive. From the corner of Vista Chino Drive and Palm Canyon Drive, head toward the mountains on Vista Chino Drive to Camino Monte Vista, go left, and then continue straight or go right on Stevens Road. This older residential area contains some beautiful examples of drought-resistant landscaping, incorporating heat-loving plants such as smoke trees, exotic cacti, and red bird-of-paradise. An especially nice side trip for those who like to garden.

right on Tahquitz Canyon Wy, then right on Museum Dr. Parking available adjacent to museum and across the street.)

The Annenberg Theater on the museum's lower level hosts concerts, drama, film, and dance. This attractive venue has seating for 430 and an ambitious schedule encompassing string quartets, ballet, modern dance, Broadway musicals, and opera performers (though unfortunately, not all at the same time). Theater tickets average $35 (box office: 760/325-4490).

Museum-sponsored nature hikes (760/325-0189 or 760/325-7186) offer a fun double-whammy of exercise and education. Led by experienced guides, these hikes range from 2 to 10 miles and are rated Easy, Moderate, Strenuous, or Very Strenuous, depending on distance and terrain. Wear sturdy, already-broken-in shoes or hiking boots; bring a hat; and carry plenty of water. Hikers meet at the museum parking lot, then form carpools to various trailheads. Hikes are held Wednesday and Saturday at 9am, except during the summer months, and cost $2 for members and $4 for nonmembers.

 Palm Springs Villagefest. This weekly street fair is *the* place to be on Thursday nights, when Palm Canyon Drive closes to car traffic between Amado and Baristo Streets, and vendors set up booths for a huge open-air market. A certified farmers market offers fresh produce and armloads of flowers, while merchandise ranges from one-of-a-kind jewelry to local musicians' CDs to *objets d'art* from throughout the state.

Services include chair massage, acupressure, even advice: We've seen tarot card readers and financial advisors as well as an "Ask the Rabbi" booth. Browsing is welcome, and you don't need to buy to have a great time; lots of people simply park themselves at the streetside restaurants and watch the human parade. This event is as much a neighborhood social as a chance to shop—a gossipfest about who's doing what with whom; which restaurants are hot or not, and who's selling the tastiest strawberries at the best price. One end of the fair is devoted to kids, with towering inflatable slides and (at least during the summer) a cool maze for chasing around with SuperSoakers (760/320-3781; open 6–10pm, Oct–May, 7–10pm June–Sept; admission is free).

Taste of history. Step back—waaaay back—in time at the Village Green Heritage Center (221 S Palm Canyon Dr; 760/323-8297). Operated by the Palm Springs Historical Society, the Heritage Center surrounds a minipark with its array of several old buildings, including the McCallum Adobe (1884), the oldest remaining building in the area. Relocated and restored, this adobe serves as a museum of photos, clothes, tools, books, and other artifacts from 19th–century Palm Springs. In the same complex, "Miss Cornelia's Little House," constructed of railroad ties and purchased by sisters Cornelia and Florilla White in 1913, and a well-stocked replica of a general store offer another taste of the city long before it became a mecca of movie stars and money.

Movie star fashions. Ready for your closeup, dahling? You will be after a trip to Celebrity Seconds, a "gently used" clothing store that sells clothes once worn by the stars. Owner Arlyn Rudolph says, "It's like shopping in the wardrobe department at MGM," and indeed, the racks are dripping with designer items worn by Ginger Rogers, Ann Margret, Julie Andrews, and many more. The largest collection of items comes from Ginger Rogers—hats, gloves, shawls, evening wear, and shoes (the latter in sizes 6 through 8; perhaps those dance numbers left her feet a bit swollen by the end of the day). The vintage clothing selection dates back to the 1930s and includes some marvelous costume jewelry. (333 N Palm Canyon Dr; 760/416-2072; closed Tues; summer schedule varies, so call ahead.) Note: Rudolph also owns Unique Repeat, a high-end consignment store with such labels as

Valentino and Escada (73-739 Hwy 111, Palm Desert; 760/340-4411; open Mon–Sat).

Dog park. Canine companions are welcome to play leash-free in this cherished community park, which is completely enclosed. Along with a separate fenced-off area for small dogs, the facility has all the necessities: grass, trees, pooper-scoopers, fire hydrants, and drinking fountains. It's supported completely by private donations, so express your gratitude by cleaning up after your pup (222 Civic Dr N, behind City Hall; 760/332-8362; open every day).

Blowin' in the wind. As you near Palm Springs from the west on Interstate 10, you'll see windmills—thousands of them—sprouting like a garden of pinwheels across hillsides and valleys. They're not drilling for oil or blowing smog away from the valley; they're busy generating electricity for our power-thirsty state. Join Wind Farm Tours, Inc., for a tour of these alternative energy sources on an ecologically correct, wind-and-solar-powered electric vehicle. The 90-minute narrated trips wind through the surreal forests of towering two- and three-bladed windmills like some ultramodern version of a walk in the woods. Forgive us for saying you'll be blown away by all the information provided by the guides. Reservations highly recommended; tour times vary by season. The tour site is located at Interstate 10 at Indian Avenue, on the north side frontage road about 1¼ miles west of Indian Avenue; 760/251-1997; adults, $23; seniors, $20, students (high school and college) $15, kids, $10; www.windmill tours.com.

Eco-tours. Here's one of those trendy eco-adventure trips that doesn't require airfare to Costa Rica or the Amazon. Desert Adventures (67-555 E Palm Canyon Dr, Cathedral City; 760/324-JEEP or 888/440-JEEP; www.red-jeep.com) provides several jeep tours throughout the region, pairing sightseeing with tons of info about local geology and botany, desert wildlife, and Indian culture. For international visitors, the company offers narration in Spanish, German, French, and Italian as well as English. Trips, undertaken in jaunty red jeeps that seat seven passengers, range from a journey up the Santa Rosa Mountains to an exploration of the San Andreas Fault. Some of the drives include stops for hiking; people with limited walking ability or other health concerns should check with the tour operators for details. All hikers and walkers should wear enclosed walking shoes; sandals and cactus spines are a bad mix. Prices range from $69 to $129, with a discount for kids (must be over 6) and seniors.

Belay on! The Uprising Rock Climbing Center (1500 S Gene Autry Trail; 760/320-6630 or 888/CLIMB-ON; www.uprising.com) attracts both beginning and experienced climbers with rugged, man-made surfaces offering 125 different routes. The "rocks" here are shade-covered and misted—a real bonus on one of the desert's 350 sunny days. Climb all day for $15, or take an introductory class with the rest of the day for climbing for $36, including equipment.

Celebrity tours. For lots of folks, the appeal of Palm Springs lies largely in its star-studded past—and its current status as a retreat for the wealthy and the well known. Would-be stargazers have two options. One, buy a map of past and current celebrity homes at the Palm Springs Visitors Information Center (approx. $5) and go for a walking and driving tour on your own. (Two highlights: Liberace resided at 501 Belardo Rd; Frank Sinatra's Twin Palms home is at 1148 Alejo.) Two, hop on a bus: Celebrity Tours (760/770-2700) offers one- or two-hour tours, complete with narration, history, and the occasional juicy tidbit. This trip focuses mainly on the big names of the past—you'll pass the former homes of Liberace, Frank Sinatra, and Jack Benny—but also features present-day residents like Kurt Russell and Goldie Hawn. Reservations are required. The one-hour tour is $18 for adults, $15 for seniors, and $8 for students and kids 16 and under. Special tours (including access to a particular home) may be arranged with advance notice.

"Where are all the celebrities? I haven't seen any yet!"—an impatient young woman, newly arrived in Palm Springs, walking into the Visitors Information Center near Tramway Road.

Elvis slept here. And so can you. Rent a "celebrity house" by the day, week, or month through McLean Company Rentals (760/322-2500 or 800/777-4606; www.ps4rent.com). Available properties include Liberace's former compound (five bedrooms, seven bathrooms) and a hillside home once owned by Elvis Presley. The company Web site offers a comprehensive list, complete with prices and 360-degree-view pictures.

Architecturally speaking. Part of Palm Springs's visual élan comes from its abundance of classic buildings dating from the later 1940s through the '60s. Houses that could be purchased for a low five figures 30 years ago are now well into the six-digit range, and several of the architects involved have become famous figures. One, the late Albert Frey, was a disciple of Le Corbusier who partnered with other area architects to design Palm Springs's landmarks like Palm Springs City Hall (1957) and the Palm Springs Aerial Tramway Valley Station (1963). He was also the creative genius behind the Tramway Oasis Gas Station (2901 N Palm Canyon Dr, at the intersection of N Palm Canyon and Tramway Road). This one-of-a-kind modernist structure with soaring roofline was recently restored and transformed into an art gallery called Montana St. Martin (760/323-7183; open Tues–Sun except during summer, when it's open by appointment).

For another glimpse of vintage Frey, take Palm Canyon Drive to Tahquitz Canyon Way and turn right (toward the mountains) to the end of the street. Nestled into the mountain above the impressive stone Burgess Estate is the small glass-and-metal refuge the artist built for himself (it's now owned by the Desert Museum). Constructed in 1964, the spare, angular home is known for the enormous boulder that dominates its living spaces.

Richard Neutra, another groundbreaking modernist and contemporary of Frey's, built a home nearby that's also worth a pilgrimage. Constructed in 1947 for the same man who owned Frank Lloyd Wright's Fallingwater in Pennsylvania, the so-called Kaufmann house fell into disrepair during the '60s but has been painstakingly restored. It's near the end of Vista Chino Road on West Chino Canyon Road.

Finally, there's Bob Hope's futuristic home at the top of Southridge Drive (take E Palm Canyon Dr east past Araby Dr, over a dry riverbed, and then look up the hill). It's the one on top of a hill that looks a bit like a manta ray or a portobello mushroom, with a distinctive curving roof. Designed by John Lautner, the house is used mainly for fund-raising parties now, since the Hopes live most of the time at their main residence, 1188 El Alameda.

One Albert Frey building has become a popular clothing-optional hotel, the Terra Cotta Inn. Formerly known as the Monkey Tree, the 17-room complex at 2388 E Racquet Club Road was

GET YOUR KICKS . . .

. . . on Route 66! So the famed song goes, and today thousands of travelers still venture into Southern California intent on driving at least part of the original "Mother Road" immortalized by author John Steinbeck in The Grapes of Wrath. *Many are Europeans, and one wonders what they think of America as they stop at roadside cafes to savor a greasy burger and fries as if these were foods of the gods. In truth, the transcontinental icon known as Route 66 (it actually runs from Chicago to Santa Monica) has been mostly swallowed by the interstate highway system. Significant stretches remain across Southern California between the Pacific Ocean and Needles on the California/Arizona border, but you'll need a guidebook to trace its path: State and county maps are of little help, since they usually don't show the number 66 at all. The best guide is* Route 66 Traveler's Guide and Roadside Companion *(St. Martin's Griffin, New York, 2nd ed., 1995) by Tom Snyder, founder of the nonprofit US Route 66 Association (PO Drawer 5323, Oxnard, CA 93031). A $20 one-time fee gets you a certificate and an embroidered patch, and helps support the group's efforts to raise traveler awareness and preserve the route's history and important sights. Don't have time to send away for the book? Search the Web using "Route 66," and you'll find countless sites devoted to maps, directions, and recommendations.*

designed by Frey in 1960. The current owners purchased the building in 1995, renamed it the Terra Cotta, and converted it to a hotel where the clientele can enjoy the sun and stars *au naturel*. It offers extra-spacious rooms, a mountain-view Jacuzzi, and free breakfast served by the pool (760/322-6059 or 800/786-6938; terracottainn.com).

Annual Film Fest. Cinephiles wouldn't dream of missing the lively Nortel Palm Springs International Film Fest held each January. While the Sundance Film Festival in Utah may get more press, this rapidly growing event is winning praise for the quality and quantity of its screenings, including a terrific selection of foreign films. In fact, this fest hosts the international submissions of Best Foreign Film for Academy Award consideration.

If all this '50s style architecture puts you in the mood to shop, pick up an authentic piece of the decade at John's Resale Furnishings (891 N Palm Canyon Dr; 760/416-8876). It's a favorite of interior designers and others searching for just the right vintage dinette, Charles Eames chair, or kidney-shaped coffee table.

Started in 1989, Palm Springs's version of Cannes draws an international crowd, with plenty of directors and actors in the mix along with enthusiastic, knowledgeable spectators. Notable attendees at the 2000 festival included Annette Bening and Warren Beatty, Catherine Deneuve, and Pedro Almodovar. Along with the feature film festival in the winter, which includes older films as well as world premieres, a series of short films (including video and animation) is offered each August. Venues and ticket prices vary. For information contact 760/322-2930 or 800/898-7256; www.psfilmfest.org.

Palm Springs Air Museum. One of the city's don't-miss attractions, this museum is home to an impressive collection of some of the world's last examples of still-operable World War II aircraft, including the famous Flying Fortress with its ball turret nose. Want to hear some war stories to go along with the visuals? Talk to the museum volunteers—many served in WWII and have fascinating, courageous tales to share. If you're lucky, you can watch history take flight during one of the flying demonstrations of the vintage aircraft. These demos aren't scheduled daily, so be sure to call the museum ahead of time to find out what's flying when.

An exhibition of period automobiles adds another dimension to this step-back-in-time experience, as do the daily movies on topics such as the Tuskegee Airmen. The recently remodeled and expanded museum is available for private parties of 100 to 3,500 guests, by the way, in case you'd like to tie the knot or have a birthday party among the propellers (745 N Gene Autry Trail, on the north side of the Palm Springs International Airport; 760/778-6262; open every day; $7.50 for adults, $6 for seniors, $3.50 for kids 6–12; www.air-museum.org).

Red hot blues. For fans of jazz and the blues, the Blue Guitar (120 S Palm Canyon Dr, second floor; 760/327-1549) is the top venue in town, with live music in an intimate, cozy setting. The house band is hot, and so are the various guest artists who drop in (open Thurs–Sat nights; full bar; call for reservations).

Horse sense. Take in the sights from a Western saddle with one of the guided horseback tours offered by Smoke Tree Stables (2500 Toledo Ave; 760/327-1372). Routes feature views of the mountains, desert, and Indian Canyons. The stables close during the summer and traditionally reopen on Labor Day. One-hour rides, $30; two-hour rides, $55. Call for reservations.

Palm Springs by bike. Exploring the city via bicycle is a great way to cruise through neighborhoods or take to the mountain trails. The Bighorn Bicycle Rental Tour Company (302 N Palm Canyon Dr; 760/325-3367) has hourly and daily rental rates in addition to guided bike treks. The latter features rides to Indian Canyons and a celebrity home tour. Another rental outfit, Adventure Bike Tours (760/328-0282), offers conventional bicycles as well as Lee Iacocca's E-Bike, powered by a small electric motor. The rental companies supply maps; you can also get a free map of several routes through Palm Springs online (www.palmsprings.com/city/palmsprings/bikemap.html). Don't worry much about getting lost: The city has also posted numerous "bike route" signs throughout town.

Pottery classes. Kneading cool, slippery clay and then fashioning it into a vase or bowl is a fun, even spiritual, endeavor. If you've never tried it before, Palm Springs Pottery (198 S Indian Canyon Dr; 760/322-6584) offers beginning classes, either as a series or in a one-day "camp" geared to visitors. Facilities include six electric wheels (a much easier alternative to the self-powered kick wheel), numerous glazes, and two kilns. The one-day lessons, in which teachers demonstrate how to throw pots and supervise your work, cost $20 per hour if you don't want to keep any pieces; $30 an hour if you'd like to have your work glazed, fired, and mailed to you (postage is extra). Even people who don't want to get their hands dirty should enjoy this shop, which offers traditional and modern pottery for sale as well as the chance to watch pieces being made. Minimum age for taking classes is 13.

Channel your inner artiste with one of the ongoing courses at the Desert Fine Arts Academy, located at 1103 N Palm Canyon Drive. Classes for teens and adults include painting, drawing, and sculpture; special programs are available for kids. Information: 760/320-6806.

Up, up, and away. Hot air balloon rides, held at dusk or dawn, are a favorite pastime both of visitors who seek a different vantage point of the landscape and locals celebrating a birthday or other special occasion. Balloon Above the Desert is open September to May (760/776-5785 or 800/342-8506; batd@gte.net; pshotairballoons.com). Dream Flights operates October to May (760/321-5154 or 800/933-5628; info@dream flights.com; www.dreamflights.com).

DESERT CASINOS

Look out, Las Vegas. The Indian-owned casinos in the Coachella Valley are hoping to give you a run for your money.

When voters legalized Nevada-style gaming on California Indian tribal lands, they opened the door for a major boom in casino gambling. The new laws meant that, among other changes, the casinos could replace video-style games that rewarded winners with a receipt that had to be exchanged for cash with real coin-dispensing slot machines.

Tribes in the Palm Springs region are both expanding existing casinos and building new ones. The Agua Caliente tribe has said it will spend about $150 million to renovate and expand its Spa Casino in downtown Palm Springs, and is also budgeting an estimated $80 million to build a new casino in Thousand Palms near Rancho Mirage. The latter is at the corner of Ramon Road and Bob Hope Drive, just off Interstate 10. Other casinos scheduled for massive renovation are the Fantasy Springs in Indio and the Spotlight 29 in Coachella.

Like most topics in the valley, with a community that includes the young, the old, the conservative, the liberal, the extremely wealthy, and the working poor, the subject of Indian gaming and local casinos is a hot one. Supporters welcome the recreational aspects of the casinos, as well as the job opportunities and enormous revenues they generate. Critics point to the possibility of increased traffic and crowds, gaudy neon signs and bright lights, and the social problems of gambling addiction.

Fabulous Follies. The historic Plaza Theatre hosts the long-running Fabulous Palm Springs Follies from November through May. Featured performers include the "legendary line of long-legged lovelies," a group of high-kicking, high-spirited women ranging from 50-plus to 80-something. Most are retired professional entertainers who show little evidence of having slowed down since their Broadway days. Depending on their age, patrons think the show is either swell or pure blue-haired camp; either way, it's a local institution (128 S Indian Canyon Dr; 760/327-0225; www.psfollies.com; ticket prices are in the $37–$65 range).

In addition to video poker and slot machines, casinos offer card games such as poker and blackjack as well as bingo and other games. Most are open 24 hours a day, seven days a week. Some, like the Fantasy Springs Casino, offer additional attractions such as concerts and boxing matches. One caution: The casinos themselves tend to be heavy on cigarette smoke, although some have nonsmoking areas.

Casinos in the Palm Springs area include:

Casino Morongo, 49-750 Seminole Drive, Cabazon (off I-10 west of Palm Springs); 800/252-4499. Located near the Desert Hills factory outlet stores, this casino offers valet parking and a gift shop. Open 24 hours every day.

Fantasy Springs Casino, 84-245 Indio Springs Road, Indio (off I-10 at Golf Center Parkway); 760/342-5695 or 800/827-2946. This casino also has a bowling alley and books a number of big-name concert acts. Open 24 hours every day.

Spa Casino, 140 N Indian Canyon Drive at Tahquitz Canyon Way, Palm Springs; 760/323-5865 or 800/258-2WIN. Just think: If you lose money, you can always go book a soothing massage at the spa next door. Open 24 hours every day.

Spotlight 29 Casino, 46-200 Harrison, Coachella (at Dillon Rd and I-10); 760/775-5566. Entertainment options include boxing matches and concerts. Open 24 hours every day.

 Water world. Oasis Waterpark isn't just for kids, although during the summer it may seem that every kid in the desert is zipping down one of the 13 waterslides or Boogie boarding at the wave-action pool. A great spot for families, there are minislides for the smallest kids, a 70-foot free-fall slide for braver souls, and an easygoing inner-tube float perfect for stressed-out adults. A health club beckons would-be muscle builders, while beach cabanas with waiter service are custom-made for the slothful. Lifeguards and first-aid staff are on duty; lockers, showers, and changing rooms are available; food and other refreshments are for sale. You're not allowed to bring your own coolers, food, beverages, beach chairs, and so on. The park is open daily March to October. General admission is $19.95, with considerable discounts for seniors, kids, and the military (1500 Gene Autry Trail; 760/327-0499 or 800/247-4664; take E Palm Canyon Dr to Gene Autry Trail and go north).

Go hog wild. Rumble down the city streets or backcountry highways on the ultimate two-wheeler—rent a Harley-Davidson from Eaglerider (19345 N Indian Ave, Ste. LL; 760/251-5990 or 877/736-8243; psp@eaglerider.com; www.eaglerider.com). Rates average $135 per day or $900 per week for your choice of several models, including the Electra Glide, Heritage Softail Classic, and Fat Boy. A few restrictions apply: You must be at least 21 and have a valid driver's license with motorcycle endorsement from your country or state of permanent residence. The agency is open every day 9am to 5pm. Guided tours available by advance arrangement.

Bargains! The magic words "outlet shopping" draw label-conscious consumers from all over the world to the Desert Hills Premium Outlets, just a 15-minute drive west of Palm Springs in Cabazon. This Spanish-style complex is home to about 120 stores, most of them featuring famous brand names or prominent designers. The amount of savings can vary widely from one store to the next, and savvy shoppers will notice that many of the fashions are a season or so behind. Still, this is a fun place to browse or buy, especially if you know your labels and retail prices.

Some of our favorite stores: the Movado watch outlet (which features discounts on discontinued models or watches with scarcely perceptible flaws); Ermenegildo Zegna (men's clothing from a top Italian designer, at about the same prices you'd pay in Italy, which means a saving of around 25 percent); the Gap Outlet (who can tell this season's jeans from last?); the Nike Factory store (ditto for shoes); and Villeroy and Boch china. If you don't like crowds, try to visit the outlet in summer or during the week; weekends can be jammed with busloads of shoppers (48-400 Seminole Dr, Cabazon; 909/849-5018; open every day; take Hwy 10 west from Palm Springs and exit on Fields Rd or Apache Trail).

Annual White Party. "Thousands of beautiful boys danc-
ing with their shirts off"—that's how one perennial party
attendee describes Palm Springs's biggest and best gay party of
the year. The four-day affair, part of a national White Party circuit, features dances, DJs, laser shows, live performances, endless
rounds of parties, and high-spirited fun pretty much round the
clock. It's celebrated around Easter every year; in April 2000,
more than 22,000 guests attended.

Official host hotels (which usually sponsor cocktail parties,
get-togethers, and dances to supplement the main White Party at
the Convention Center) generally include the Palm Springs
Hilton and the nearby Marquis. Reserve rooms well ahead if
you're not planning to stay with friends. Tickets available for individual events or in packages; contact Jeffrey Sanker Presents
(323/653-0800; www.jeffreysanker.com) for more information.

Indulge yourself. The city abounds with salons and spas;
one of the most inviting is the Face Place (133 La Plaza;
760/325-7055). Beyond the fragrant storefront, which offers aro-
matic oils, herbal soaps, and other potions for sale, are four quiet
little casitas where facials, massages, pedicures, and other treatments are available. Soothing music, soft lighting, scented candles, and experienced practitioners will leave even the most
tightly wound Type A feeling pleasantly limp. Located on La Plaza
in the center of downtown, the Face Place feels miles away from
the downtown bustle just steps away. Open Mon to Sat during
peak season; check for summer hours.

RESTAURANTS

THE BURGER FACTORY   ☆

Chat with the customer seated next to you at the counter in
this 1960s-feeling burger joint, and you might discover he's
driven down from Hollywood for the day—and for the
burger. The mainstay menu item here is the Kong—a massive one-pound flattened softball of ground beef char-
grilled and hugged by lettuce, tomato, onion, Thousand
Island dressing, pickle, and a big bun. Their Hunk-Uh-
Hunk-of-Burning-Love/Elvis Burger stacks ground beef,
ham, pastrami, bacon, and grilled onions between slices of

Most locals and visitors agree: The best margarita in Palm Springs is mixed at the Blue Coyote Grill (445 N Palm Canyon Dr; 760/327-1196).

grilled sourdough bread. The Great Balls of Fire/Jerry Lee Lewis Burger is nearly aflame with three different hot sauces and jalapeño peppers in addition to the usual burger accoutrements. Decor here reflects owner Louise Reymer's penchant for Elvis-this and Elvis-that, as well as pictures of celebrity customers such as rapper/actor Ice Cube. Turkey burgers and veggie burgers are also excellent. The really cool thing about the Burger Factory? Its hours: It stays open until 4am Friday and Saturday nights. *333 S Indian Canyon Dr, Palm Springs; 760/322-7678; $; no credit cards; no checks; lunch, dinner every day; beer and wine; reservations not necessary; www.burgerfactory.com; nearest cross streets Baristo Rd and Ramon Rd.* &

CANYON BISTRO ★★

Stylish without being pretentious, this downtown restaurant is the perfect destination for those "in-between" occasions, when you want to go somewhere upscale but not at all fussy. The little sister of Le Vallauris nearby and Le St. Germain in Indian Wells, Canyon Bistro has a great pedigree without being quite as pricey. Decorated in contemporary bistro style, it sports tidy white tablecloths, open-beamed ceilings, original paintings, and a fireplace in one corner. The small bar area, with its granite counter and mirrored back walls, is a nice place to alight for a quick bite and a drink (though it can be elbow-to-elbow during peak season, while guests wait for tables); there's also patio seating for about 60 (Bonus: It's misted during the summer months). Chef Raul Garcia capably handles an international menu, which means French standards such as rotisserie chicken (which is excellent) and *pommes frites* share billing with designer pizzas, lamb curry, and tangy seafood ceviche. A pairing of mushroom-stuffed ravioli and garlicky pesto is outstanding, as is the Caesar salad. Special kudos to the wine list, which, while not extensive, offers some luscious, little-known bottles discovered by the wine-savvy management. Service is affable yet professional. *415 N Palm Canyon Dr, Palm Springs; 760/322-8664; $$; AE, DC, MC, V; no checks; lunch, dinner every day; full bar; reservations recommended; near Amado Rd.* &

COLD STONE CREAMERY

The customer's always right at this bright little ice cream parlor, where the motto is "If you can dream it, we can ice cream it!" Here's how it works: Choose one of the extra-smooth ice creams or frozen yogurts as a starting point; top flavors include strawberry, sweet cream, cheesecake, and double Dutch chocolate. Then, get creative with a choice of 40 mix-ins: graham crackers, Heath candy bars, peanuts, Oreo cookies, strawberries, Gummi Bears, even Ding Dongs. The counter person places the whole delicious mess on a frosty granite slab (the cold stone, get it?) to be chopped, mixed, and blended, then heaped onto a freshly made waffle cone. Stumped for ideas? Check out the list of "Tried and True Favorites" that cites such masterpieces as Bonnie's Snowball: chocolate ice cream, flaked coconut, brownies, and marshmallows. A small cone goes for $2.69. *155 S Palm Canyon Dr, Palm Springs; 760/327-5243; $; cash only; dessert only; no alcohol; no reservations; between Tahquitz Canyon Wy and McCallum Wy.* &

KAISER GRILLE ★★

You won't find Wiener schnitzel at Kaiser Grille. Named for owner Kaiser Morcus, the restaurant exemplifies a new energy and spirit in the Coachella Valley that make some of the more haute valley restaurants seem stuffy. Here you'll find the clientele a little more bare-shouldered, the collars a little more open, and the laughter a little louder than in the clubbier valley restaurants where geriatric decorum rules the evening. At the downtown Palm Springs location, two open-air dining terraces jut into the sidewalk like the prows of twin ships. During blast-furnace summer months, micro-misters up in the metal-finned roofline cool diners with their wispy fog. At night, diners see (and are seen by) a constant parade of passersby, but the food commands center stage. Prime rib arrives in a thick fork-tender slab (it can also be ordered blackened, Cajun style). Fish lovers have the unusual option of a "mixed grill" showcasing three different fillets. Sauces are rich, and often based on a classic beurre blanc flavored with either mango or local citrus juices. Grilled steak is a specialty, served with heaps of fresh

It's a tradition:
Desert visitors need
to sample a date
shake. Stop by
Hadley's Fruit
Orchards, just east
of the Desert Hills
Premium Outlets in
Cabazon, for one of
these delicious milk
shakes made with
naturally sweet
dates. Although
there are no
orchards here,
Hadley's sells an
amazing variety of
nuts, dates, dried
fruits, and trail
mix; there's also a
deli and lots of
free samples for
snacking.

steamed vegetables and mashed potatoes. The only thing better than sitting outside is sitting inside, where you can see the activity in the huge, open kitchen. There is a second location in Palm Desert. *205 S Palm Canyon Dr, Palm Springs; 760/323-1003; 74225 Hwy 111, Palm Desert; 760/779-1988; $$; AE, DC, DIS, MC, V; no checks; lunch, dinner every day; full bar; reservations recommended; corner of Arenas Rd.* &

LAS CASUELAS TERRAZA ★

Started in 1958 by Florencio and Mary Delgado, Las Casuelas has been a downtown Palm Springs institution virtually from the beginning. President Dwight Eisenhower was a regular customer, fueling up on Mary's tamales after his golf rounds. Liz Taylor, George Montgomery, Bob Hope, and Dinah Shore all plunked down for big combination plates of enchiladas, tacos, and burritos. The liveliest of their three locations, Las Casuelas Terraza draws its energy off the heavy foot traffic of Palm Canyon Drive. A big palapa-fringed bar and patio open to the street, and live music pumps out from here as strongly as the straight shots of aged tequilas. If you love black beans Oaxacan style, you'll enjoy the black bean "pizza" (really a tostada) with chicken. Unfortunately, Las Casuelas in general seems to have succumbed to too many tourist requests for mildness and offers few dishes that capture a sense of authenticity or innovation. (One of the burrito styles is rather odd and bland, loaded with diced potatoes and celery.) So why come here? For the Spanish Colonial decor, the crowd, the indoor-outdoor feel, the music, and the great location. Additional locations at Las Casuelas The Original (368 N Palm Canyon Dr, Palm Springs; 760/325-3213), and Las Casuelas Nuevas (70-050 Highway 111, Rancho Mirage; 760/328-8844). *222 S Palm Canyon Dr, Palm Springs; 760/325-2794; $$; AE, DC, DIS, MC, V; no checks; lunch, dinner every day; full bar; reservations recommended; at Arenas Rd.* &

LE PEEP ★★

With its bright, welcoming interior and amiable servers, this casual restaurant is a great place to start the day. Although Le Peep serves a creditable lunch, it's breakfast and brunch that rule the roost. Eggs are a specialty, arriving poached, scrambled, as omelets, or in hearty skillet dishes layered with potatoes, meats, cheese, or vegetables. Cholesterol-watchers can take the Great "Lite" Way, a choice of four omelets prepared with egg whites. There's even a combo worthy of Monty Python: the Lumberjack Breakfast, a feast of pancakes, potatoes, bacon or sausage, and of course, eggs. Light, fluffy Belgian waffles are another good bet (ask them to "hold the snow" if you don't want powdered sugar), as are the pancakes made with granola or blueberries. Service is swift, but it's OK to linger and chat in the comfortable booths or well-spaced tables, so have another cappuccino or latte. *2665 E Palm Canyon Dr, Palm Springs; 760/416-1444; $; AE, DIS, MC, V; no checks; breakfast, lunch every day; no alcohol; no reservations; www.lepeep. com; at Farrell Dr.*

LE VALLAURIS ★★★

Named for the small town in the south of France where Picasso took to making pottery later in life, Le Vallauris successfully combines uncompromising elegance with the informality of dining alfresco. The restaurant occupies a historic ranch house not far from the hubbub of Palm Canyon Drive (but seemingly a world apart), its ficus-shaded exterior almost too understated—except for the covey of valet-parked Rollses and Mercedeses. Step through the door, however, and you're in a magical setting of indoor and outdoor spaces. The patio capitalizes on Palm Springs's fabulous winter weather. Outdoor tables are set with linens and fine china, and with stars overhead, cool night air, and candles aglow you sense that this is indeed a special dining space. Interior rooms are equally pleasing, with draped alcoves and fine paintings. Belgian-born owner Paul Bruggeman earned his stars operating St. Germain on Melrose Avenue in Los Angeles (the site now occupied by equally famed Patina), and the menu, overseen by executive chef Jean-Paul Lair, reflects Bruggeman's love of what he calls "contemporary French/Mediterranean" cuisine—with some Southwest overtones befitting his 40 years in Southern California. The menu is an extravagant journey.

Breakfast lovers, take note: Billy Reed's serves omelets, eggs Benedict, corned beef hash, oatmeal, and other eye-openers all day long. Pancakes and waffles are served until 3pm. The sprawling restaurant is a little heavy on the red velvet decor, but the prices are decent and service is swift. (1800 N Palm Canyon Dr; 760/325-1946; open every day 7am–11pm.)

One can start with beluga caviar, or terrine of foie gras, or light, crisp crab cakes with whole-grain mustard sauce. Lamb lovers will yield willingly to a perfectly roasted rack, well seasoned in the classic manner with garlic and thyme, or, at lunch, to the more adventuresome marinated grilled lamb loin with sesame sauce. The veal chop with pommes soufflés is one of Southern California's best. The fish here, either seared or sautéed, accompanied by inventive sauces such as a citrus dressing or red chili sauce, is so buttery and fresh it seems the ocean must be nearly next door. *385 W Tahquitz Canyon Wy, Palm Springs; 760/325-5059 or 888/525-5852; $$$; AE, DC, DIS, MC, V; no checks; lunch, dinner every day, brunch Sun (dinner only Thurs–Mon in summer); full bar; reservations recommended; vallauris@aol.com; www.levallauris.com; from Palm Canyon Dr go 3 blocks toward the mountains on W Tahquitz Canyon Wy.* &

ST. JAMES AT THE VINEYARD ★★★

Palm Springs's most interesting dinner menu fuses Pacific Rim, French, Indian Ocean, and American steak house cuisines in a unique style born of owner James Offord's love of travel. Former chef Johannes Bacher has moved on, and chef Michael Hutchings has moved into the kitchen. By all accounts, the restaurant's as good as ever. Appetizers change often, but we hope to see more of the coconut-milk steamed mussels and assorted satays with green papaya salad. As for entrees, St. James remains rightfully famous for its curries—lamb, chicken, shrimp, or vegetable— served with traditional condiments and basmati rice. Other standouts include a stir-fried lobster tail over couscous (very pricey), a grilled lamb rack with vanilla-infused reduction, or a fabulous Bouillabaisse Burmese that immerses a bounty of seafood in a sauce enlivened with ginger, pineapple, lime juice, and cardamom. After all these flavors you'll probably be too exhausted for dessert. Service is attentive but unhurried; feel free to enjoy a meal that will last several hours. The bar, featuring almost a hundred folk art masks on the walls, is downtown's most sophisticated watering hole, and the restaurant's wine list boasts a *Wine Spectator* Award of Excellence. *265 S Palm Canyon Dr, Palm Springs;*

760/320-8041; $$$; AE, DC, DIS, MC, V; no checks; dinner every day in high season (closed on Mon during summer); full bar; reservations recommended; www.st-james.com; in the rear of the Vineyard shopping center. ♿

SHERMAN'S DELI ⭐

You want good deli, they got good deli. This no-frills dining room lacks much in the way of decor, but that's not an issue when the food is heaped high, tastes great, and doesn't cost a bundle. This kosher-style deli proves that breakfast may indeed be the most important meal of the day, with an amazing number of choices. There aren't too many places in the desert whipping up traditional matzo brie, scrambled eggs with onions, smoked whitefish, and Nova Scotia lox alongside omelets, Belgian waffles, French toast, and corned beef hash seven days a week. Lunch and dinner entrees continue the culinary hit parade with crowd pleasers like corned beef and cabbage, chicken in the pot, liver and onions, matzo ball soup, and towering sandwiches served hot or cold. As for dessert, one look in the glass case and you're a goner. The on-site bakery tempts with pastries, cheesecakes, cookies, layer cakes, and pies. Service can be perfunctory but it's generally swift, and nobody waits long for coffee refills. In addition to the large dining room with floor-to-ceiling windows, there's seating for about 40 at the sidewalk tables along Tahquitz Canyon Way. *401 Tahquitz Canyon Wy, Palm Springs; 760/325-1199; $; AE, MC, V; no checks; breakfast, lunch, dinner every day; beer and wine only; no reservations; at Indian Canyon Dr.* ♿

VINTAGE MARKET PLACE ⭐

It's a restaurant; it's a bar; it's a gourmet food shop. The Vintage Market Place wears all three hats, providing a place for casual indoor/outdoor dining, sipping vintage tequilas at the bar, or picking up the fixings for a picnic or gift basket. The retail shop has a fairly extensive selection of goodies such as fresh pastas and sauces, olive oils, condiments, cheese and pâte, beer and wine. Savvy restaurant patrons choose seating on the spacious, pleasant terrace facing Palm Canyon Drive, which provides a fine vantage point on the

Drop into the Henry Frank Arcade on Palm Canyon Drive (just across from the Hyatt, near the corner of Tahquitz Canyon Wy) and you'll find the Garden Café. The charming owner makes terrific espresso drinks—hot or iced—as well as some excellent Mediterranean snacks, such as stuffed grape leaves.

sidewalk comings and goings. Sure, the cheerful indoor dining room is comfortable enough, but isn't Palm Springs all about alfresco meals? An ambitious menu runs the gamut from all-American (an enormous Cobb salad studded with avocado and applewood-smoked bacon) to French bistro (terrific country pâté served with cornichons, olives, and chopped onions). It's most successful with simple, hearty dishes such as the chicken pesto sandwich, the Cobb or Greek salads, and the pastas. The wine list offers lots of interesting selections by the glass, and the bar takes understandable pride in its selection of hard-to-find, smooth-sippin' tequilas. *105 S Palm Canyon Dr, Palm Springs; 760/320-9000; $$; AE, MC, V; no checks; lunch, dinner every day; full bar; reservations recommended; www.vintagemarket place.com; near Tahquitz Canyon Wy.* &

LODGINGS

BALLANTINES HOTEL ★★

Given Palm Springs's affinity for all things 1950s, it's easy to see why this offbeat hotel devoted to the decade has made such a splash. Newly renovated with an unerring eye for classic kitsch, Ballantines has made headlines in publications from *Condé Nast Traveler* to *Vogue* as the Next Big Thing in Palm Springs accommodations. The hotel is small—just 14 rooms and suites—but big on personality, from the classic rotary dial telephones (remember those?) and blue astroturf sunning deck around the pool to fun atomic age furniture from Eames and Bertoia. The one-story building is constructed around a courtyard with the pool in the center, so all rooms are within steps of the water. Interiors are decorated with a wink and a nod to various celebs—Marilyn Monroe, Douglas Fairbanks Jr., and Audrey Hepburn are among those honored—or in campy themes like French Artist (*sacre bleu,* what a gaudy bedspread!). We especially like the "Women of the Movies" room, adorned with photos of actresses and a pink television. Even the TVs are tuned in to the '50s, with the in-house movie channel offering classic films of the decade as well as brilliantly bad B-movies. The hotel has a two-night minimum stay and caters to adults; free minibreakfast and newspaper included. Service is welcoming and eager to please. *1420 N Indian Canyon Dr, Palm Springs; 800/780-3464; $$; AE, MC, V; no checks; www.palmsprings.com/ballantines; at N Indian Canyon Dr and Stevens Rd.*

CASA CODY ★★★

Though it's only two blocks from the main drag, this comfy old B&B has a pleasantly cloistered feeling, with grounds surrounded by a buffer of bougainvillea. It's known as the oldest continuously operating inn in the area, starting out as an adobe home built by Harold Cody, a cousin of Buffalo Bill, during the 1920s. Later, one of the main buildings served as the quarters for General George Patton's offices during their training for the North African campaign. Today, most of the 23 accommodations are in single-story, hacienda-like buildings built around courtyards with pools, and range from small studios to one- and two-bedroom suites. Furnishings are simple, yet stylish, and several of the rooms offer wood-burning fireplaces. Chaise lounges with views of the nearby San Jacinto Mountains and the lush landscaping beckon outside every door. In addition to these rooms, the inn offers a semisecluded cottage and a classic two-bedroom adobe. The staff is friendly and down-to-earth, and while the occasional noisy guest can rattle the calm here, Casa Cody is generally as serene as a still desert night. A complimentary breakfast is served in the mornings, along with newspapers, and the tree-shaded tables near the pool make a fine place to linger over coffee, muffins, conversation, and birdsongs. *175 S Cahuilla Rd, Palm Springs; 760/320-9346; $$; AE, DIS, MC, V; checks OK; from S Palm Canyon Dr take Tahquitz Canyon Wy west to S Cahuilla Rd and turn left.*

COYOTE INN ★★

 Within walking distance of downtown Palm Springs, the Coyote Inn has all the feel of a half-century-old classic little Spanish courtyard inn—except that the spotless little Coyote is virtually brand-new. The walled and gated enclave shelters only seven tile-roofed suites, each with full kitchen

HOTELS AND
HOT SUMMER SPECIALS

Peak season in Palm Springs and the surrounding communities is pretty much October through April or May. This is when the climate is at its mildest, and the hotel prices at their highest. But as temperatures rise, prices tumble.

Hardy folk who can stand the triple-digit heat in July or August can usually find accommodations discounted as much as 50 percent, even at many of the top resorts. Also worth searching out: off-season golf packages that include unlimited rounds with the price of a room (see the Golf chapter for additional information on summer discounts at local courses).

Here are some examples of the hotel deals typically found from June into September. Unless otherwise noted, prices are for two people for one night. To find rates like these, check hotel or travel Web sites, or call the hotels and ask for their best available rates. Hint: Prices are generally lower Sun through Thurs than on weekends.

Hyatt Grand Champions, Indian Wells:

For $119—less than the usual price of a single room in high season—visitors receive a split-level, mountain- or garden-view room with balcony and unlimited rounds of golf on nearby courses—with cart included. 760/341-1000 or 800/554-9288.

(including dishwasher), library, small dining table, sitting area, fireplace, and comfortable, firm beds. Rooms all look out on the courtyard and pool, so the inn has a great sense of community (which can be a bit of a downside, however, if you're looking for privacy or anonymity). From the pool, you look straight up at the mountains, making this one of Palm Springs's best lodgings in which to enjoy the beauty of the desert. A hidden garden spa is great for a before-bed soak. *234 S Patencio Rd, Palm Springs; 760/327-0304 or 888/334-0633; $$ AE, DC, MC, V; no checks; www.springs. gardeninns.com; from Palm Canyon Dr take Arenas Rd toward the mountains and turn left on Patencio Rd.*

Indian Wells Resort Hotel, Indian Wells:

Summer rates can go as low as $59 midweek for a room with a king-size or two queen-size beds, plus a free buffet breakfast and hosted cocktail hour with free drinks and snacks. Golf packages also available. 760/345-6466 or 800/248-3220.

Two Bunch Palms, Desert Hot Springs:

This exclusive, peaceful hideaway (no cell phones allowed in public spaces, a move we applaud) that caters to the rich offers 50 percent off regular rates to first-time visitors and repeat guests during July and August. Regular rates start around $175. Two-night minimum. 760/329-8791.

Ballantines Hotel, Palm Springs:

From June 1 until September 30, rates at this homage to the 1950s go for about half price, dropping the ever-popular Marilyn Monroe suite from $255 to $155. 800/780-3464.

Desert Isle of Palm Springs, Palm Springs:

These time-share condos offer pleasant grounds and spacious, modern suites starting at around $65 during the summer, about half the winter rate. 760/327-8469 or 800/225-0584.

Marriott Desert Springs, Palm Desert:

Summer season rates can dip to $99, $89 for active military or government personnel, as opposed to winter tariffs over more than $200 per night. 760/341-1893.

DESERT ISLE OF PALM SPRINGS ★★

Actually a time-share resort, this attractive property offers spacious, nicely decorated living quarters that are suitable for couples or families (but you'll have to leave the pets at home). One- and two-bedroom suites are available, with a minimum size of about 900 square feet. Each includes a fully equipped kitchen (no need to bring your own pots or silverware), dining area, living room complete with fireplace and TV, modern bathrooms and one or two sizeable bedrooms. Lots of white furniture, light, and neutral walls create a pleasantly uncluttered feel. Patio doors lead to semiprivate sitting areas with individual barbecues and lounge chairs surrounded by well-tended lawns. Many of the accommodations here overlook one of the two pools; other recreation options include two tennis courts, a fitness center, billiards, and a palapa-sheltered Ping-Pong table. Rentals are by the night or the week. The resort is adjacent to the Le Peep restaurant, which serves a good breakfast and lunch. *2555 E Palm Canyon Dr, Palm Springs; 760/327-8469 or 800/225-0584; $$; AE, DIS, MC, V; checks OK; desertisle@interworldnet.net; www.interworldnet.net/desertisle/; at Farrell Dr.*

ESTRELLA INN AND VILLAS   ★★

Yet another fine example of updated 1930s elegance, the Estrella is one of the most romantic old hotels in the Tennis District. Refurbished a few years back to the tune of $4 million, the place where Carole Lombard and Bing Crosby once slept definitely has star quality. The four-acre property has a cloistered feel, with carefully manicured rose gardens, curving footpaths, courtyards, three pools, and classic Old California architecture. Dozens of mature fruit trees provide shade, not to mention juicy treats just a pluck away. Many of the rooms are furnished with antiques, while others have a contemporary Southwest look. Lodgings include studios, two-bedroom suites, and charming one- or two-bedroom bungalows with fireplace and kitchen. Stay in one of these pretty little villas for a honeymoon or other special occasion—or just to pretend you're a star hiding out from the adoring public. Pets are allowed here (except in the courtyards), although you'll need to pay a deposit. *415 S Belardo Rd, Palm Springs; 760/320-4117 or 800/237-3687; $$$; AE, DC, MC, V; no checks; info@estrella.com; Palm Canyon Dr to Ramon Rd, west to S Belardo Rd.*

HYATT REGENCY SUITES   ★★

 This member of a corporate chain is nowhere near as nice as the Hyatt Grand Champions in Indian Wells, but rates a mention for several reasons. The all-suite format (one or two bedrooms available) means a little extra room to spread out, since even the less-expensive rooms include a spacious sitting room with couch and a small dining table, along with the bedroom and bath. The location is prime, especially if you're in town without a car: It's walking distance to dozens of eateries, bars, shops, and attractions in the heart of downtown Palm Springs. And finally, it's big: For people who don't enjoy the more intimate B&B scene, the Hyatt offers six floors of relative anonymity. The best rooms here are on the higher floors on the side facing the mountains; suites overlooking Palm Canyon Drive can be a bit noisier, especially on VillageFest nights. There's only one pool, and a small one at that, and it's odd that a hotel of this size didn't have a voice message system for the room phones at press time. Still, it's modern and good-looking (especially the dramatic lobby atrium with bar in the center), convenient (free parking is available under the hotel, which also happens to be next door to Saks Fifth Avenue), and a great deal during the summer, when a comfortable mountain-view suite can be had for $79 per night. *285 N Palm Canyon Dr, Palm Springs; 760/322-9000 or 800/55-HYATT; $$$; AE, DC, DIS, MC, V; checks OK; www.hyatt.com; at Amado Rd.* &

INGLESIDE INN ★★★

"Garbo Slept Here" proclaims the cover of this luxury hotel's brochure, and she's just one of dozens of celebrities who have made this cushy hideaway their temporary home. Originally built as a private estate, the Ingleside was converted to an inn during the 1920s and now has 30 rooms, suites, and villas. No two accommodations are alike at this official Palm Springs Historic Landmark. Many offer fireplaces and/or private patios, while all are decorated tastefully and luxuriously with muted lighting, antiques, chandeliers, and refrigerators offering free light snacks and soft drinks. Many of the rooms face the pool area or courtyard. Despite being a block from Palm Springs's main thoroughfare, the inn has a secluded aura that makes it a popular place to recuperate from plastic surgery or simply go on retreat. Room service is offered for all meals (as is poolside service) but it would be a shame to miss the grandly old-fashioned restaurant and lounge, Melvyn's. Here, you'll see photos of owner Mel Haber (who renovated the property in 1994) posing with the rich and famous. The pictures add credence to the bar's being voted "best place to see celebrities" by local newspaper readers in 1999. The menu's as classic as the setting: hot spinach salad, oysters Rockefeller, veal Oscar, steak Diane, and, possibly, the best martinis in the valley. Lunch is served Mon through Fri, brunch Sat and Sun, dinner nightly. The lounge is open until 2am and features live jazz on Sundays. *200 W Ramon Rd, Palm Springs; 760/325-0046 or 800/772-6655; $$$; AE, DIS, MC, V; checks OK; info@inglesideinn.com; www.ingleside inn.com; take Palm Canyon Dr to Ramon Rd and go west.*

KORAKIA PENSIONE ★★★

Located on a quiet side street within walking distance of downtown, Korakia immediately transports a visitor to a Moroccan oasis. Scottish artist Gordon Courts built the white-walled, wedding-cake–like house in 1924 as a retreat and salon for his many artistic and intellectual friends. A fantasy then, it remains a grand stage set today. (A Mediterranean villa directly across the street with cocoa-brown walls, tile roof, and palm-fringed eaves has also joined the Korakia ensemble.) Current owner Doug Smith virtually invented the term "restorative designer" with his knack for making every room wildly hip; he lives in each room, waiting for his muse, before remodeling. Decor may include giant hand-carved four-poster beds draped in mosquito netting, campaign furniture, and African and Balinese influences. Smith travels the world frequently, and his inn has become a visual journal of his jaunts. Numerous fireplaces lend a magical warmth on cold winter nights. Continental breakfast is served in the walled entry patio to the full-throated accompaniment of 15 lovebirds and parakeets. Kitchenettes for light cooking are stocked with Häagen-Dazs ice cream, baguettes, and Brie, leaving one to ponder, What more does one need? *257 S Patencio Rd, Palm Springs; 760/864-6411; $$$–$$$$; no credit cards; checks OK; closed July 15–Labor Day; from Palm Canyon Dr (Hwy 111) take Arenas Rd 4 blocks west to S Patencio Rd, then left.* &

LA MANCHA PRIVATE VILLAS ★★★★

The living is easy at these luxury digs, and not just during the summertime. Situated on 20 acres of lushly landscaped, walled-in land, La Mancha is the ultimate in privacy and beauty. The grounds are gorgeously Mediterranean, with towering palm trees, red tile roofs, and an abundance of fountains. Even the least expensive patio rooms and junior suites offer private patios (some with spas), as well as minirefrigerators and microwaves. At the next level, condo-style villas feature a choice of one, two, or three bedrooms (each with its own bath), but it's the private luxury villas that are really worth a splurge. These graceful Spanish-style homes boast their own private pools and spas, along with options such as fireplaces, wet bars, and covered parking. Some even have their own tennis court. Perfect for a romantic getaway, the villas are just right for nude sunbathing; and for people who don't care to venture into town, room service is happy to set up meals indoors or by your private pool. They'll even help you put together a dinner party in your quarters. There's also a lovely dining room, the Don Quixote Club, on the premises. The secluded accommodations available here draw plenty of celebs and businessfolks who want to keep a low profile while living in high style. Some of the famous faces who've relaxed behind these walls include Robert Redford, Sally Field, Liz Taylor, and John Travolta. Currently, the entire resort is undergoing some renovation and redecorating; we expect the results to be absolutely smashing. *444 N Avenida Caballeros, Palm Springs; 760/323-1773 or 800/255-1773; $$–$$$$; AE, DC, DIS, MC, V; no checks; www.la-mancha.com; take Palm Canyon Dr or Indian Canyon Dr to Amado Rd, north to Avenida Caballeros and turn left.*

Visit Palm Springs in early December, and you might get to join the annual Christmas Hotel Walkabout. This "open house" event is hosted by a number of inns around the Tennis District (bordered by Tahquitz Canyon Wy, Ramon Rd, and Palm Canyon Dr). Held in early evening, it's a chance to socialize, check out the decorations, and tour the hotels' grounds.

MERV GRIFFIN'S RESORT HOTEL AND GIVENCHY SPA ★★★

Ooh, la la! Merv's white castle on the outskirts of town has French panache to spare. Abloom with flowers and accented with topiaries and columns, it's a little bit Hollywood and a lot Versailles. The grand foyer entrance leads through a library sitting area and smart-looking restaurant to the centerpiece of the property: the formal gardens. Here, ever-blooming flowers and neatly trimmed hedges form a geometric pattern bisected by walking paths. Beyond that

Get your poolside reading for less at used bookstores like Keep On Bookin' (611 S Palm Canyon Dr; 760/325-6200) and G. William Craig Booksellers (333 N Palm Canyon Dr; 760/323-7379).

lies an expansive rose garden and arbor, with lots of benches for seated contemplation, and a citrus orchard. Off to one side is the spa: a stately and sophisticated building with soaring ceilings, lots of natural light, and a lineup of services that includes body wraps, exotic facials, various forms of massage, hairstyling, and makeup. Guest rooms reflect that effortless chic that France pulls off so well, with soft mint greens and pinks creating a stylish, restful color scheme. Rooms facing the garden cost most, but it's well worth the money for a spacious junior suite with French doors that swing open to hundreds of roses. Although the hotel is located well away from downtown Palm Springs, that's part of the appeal. Let it be your own Petite Trianon, a getaway far from the crowds. *4200 E Palm Canyon Dr; 760/770-5000 or 800/276-5000; $$$; AE, DC, DIS, MC, V; no checks; www.merv.com; take Palm Canyon Dr to E Palm Canyon Dr to Cherokee Trail and turn left.* &

ORCHID TREE INN   ★★

There's nothing modern about this venerable lodge that dates to the 1930s, and that's just how the regulars like it. Savvy repeat visitors steer clear of the comfortable but conventional motel-style rooms in the two-story portion of the inn in favor of the homey bungalows facing a plant-filled courtyard and a pool. You could sit here for hours, watching the butterflies and hummingbirds dip and hover among the flowers while the warm scents of rosemary and citrus trees provide natural aromatherapy. (Guests are encouraged to help themselves to fresh oranges in season.) The bungalow rooms have been refurbished since their creation in 1934, and no two are alike—styles range from classic Mexican hacienda to Mission, and while some look a bit timeworn, rooms are clean and comfy. If possible, get one of the two bungalows at the end of the row facing Baristo Road: These more private accommodations offer pleasant enclosed patios, spacious sitting rooms and bedrooms, kitchenettes, and a general feeling of laid-back bonhomie. The Orchid Tree is a good place to get away from it all without being isolated, since Palm Springs's main shopping and dining district is just a brief stroll down the block. *261 S Belardo Rd,*

Palm Springs; 760/325-2791 or 800/733-3435; $$; AE, DIS, MC, V; no checks; take Palm Canyon Dr to Baristo Dr and go west to S Belardo Rd.

PALM SPRINGS MARQUIS RESORT ★

Business travelers are a main focus of this three-story, 165-room hotel near the Spa Casino and the heart of downtown. The Marquis boasts a well-equipped media room with facilities for producing videos, CDs, and computer graphics, and all guest rooms are equipped with T1 connections for laptops. Standard rooms are spacious, if a bit generic, with love seats, sizeable private balconies, ironing boards, and coffeemakers, and they're soundproofed to keep out street or next-door-neighbor noise. However, the minifridges are a pain. Not only are they noisy, they're designed to dispense and charge for beverages, snacks, and candy and can't be used to store leftovers or chill a piece of fruit. Other pesky details: lamps that wouldn't work, faulty faucets in the shower. However, the staff is pleasant, from the valets to the front desk personnel, and the proximity to shopping, dining, and attractions like the Desert Museum make the Marquis worth a mention. *150 S Indian Canyon Dr; 760/322-2121; $$; AE, MC, V; no checks; www.psmarquis.com; at Tahquitz Canyon Wy.*

THE RACQUET CLUB OF PALM SPRINGS ★★

If the walls of this classic hotel could talk, they'd be sharing some great gossip about former guests such as Marilyn Monroe, Erroll Flynn, Cary Grant, and Spencer Tracy. Founded back in 1933, this tennis club is showing its age a bit—not all of the dozen courts are in top shape, for example, although most look pretty good. But the place is brimming with history and style, from the glamour shots of celebs in the lobby to the plantation/tropical decor. It's easy to imagine Hollywood's past crème de la crème hanging out in the cocktail lounge overlooking the pool or in the secluded cottages that dot the property. Although the resort offers some two-story, condo-style lodgings, our faves are the old-fashioned hideaways named for stars. The Lana Turner has a gated, walled patio all its own, while the Rita

TENNIS, ANYONE?

Tennis has been a favorite pastime in the desert ever since actors Ralph Bellamy and Charles Farrell founded the Racquet Club in Palm Springs back in 1933. Legend has it that they were kicked off the courts at El Mirador so Marlene Dietrich could play, inspiring them to open their own club. Still open, the Racquet Club is now a resort with a dozen courts and a rich history of former players that includes Erroll Flynn, Cary Grant, Lucille Ball, Desi Arnaz, and William Powell.

Every bit as much a celebrity game as golf, tennis attracted Hollywood stars back then to the Coachella Valley, and still beckons top name players today. Tournaments draw hard-hitting participants and enthusiastic spectators at every level from the local clubs to the national circuit. And a spectacular new tennis complex has brought the game's popularity up yet another notch. For racqueteers, the opening of the Indian Wells Tennis Gardens in March 2000 was a monumental event, and not just because it meant more courts to enjoy. The big news was that the $77 million facility became the new home of the Tennis Master Series Indian Wells Tournament—a major circuit event that attracts the cream of the tennis crop. Pete Sampras, Martina Hingis, and Venus and Serena Williams were on hand to compete in the facility, which features a dramatic, spacious stadium designed by the same firm that created the Arthur Ashe Tennis Center at the U.S. Open in New York. With seating for 16,000 spectators, and 44 luxury suites, this new stadium replaces the one at the Hyatt Grand Champions as the largest in the area. Indeed, this impressive new facility is one of the biggest and best in the United States. Daily ticket prices for the tournament, which is held every March, range from $15 to $60, depending on location and time of day (ticket information: 800/999-1585; masters-series.com/indianwells/).

The private tennis club isn't open for public play; memberships run about $1,500 per year. In addition to special ticket offers for the Master Series tournament, members have access to 20 courts (including several night-lighted practice courts), an elegant lounge, and lots of social activities. "We want to be like a country club for tennis players," says spokesman Ron Gilman, adding that plans are in the works for a culinary academy here *as well. 78-200 Miles Avenue, Indian Wells; 760/341-2757 or 800/999-1585. Take Highway 111 to Miles Avenue N.*

Now, for visitors who would rather hit than sit, here's a selection of tennis facilities available for public play.

Hyatt Grand Champions Resort
44-650 Indian Wells Ln, Indian Wells
Tennis club: 760/341-2582

Before the Indian Wells Tennis Gardens stadium was built, the Hyatt's 11,500-seat stadium was the largest tennis venue in the Coachella Valley. It still hosts a number of tournaments and special events. In addition to the stadium, the Hyatt has a dozen lighted courts available (hard court, clay, and grass) for play, as well as ball machines, private or semiprivate lessons, and a pro shop. Check with the hotel about corporate tennis packages. Court rental fees are $20 per hour for hard courts, $30 per hour for clay or grass. Take Highway 111 to Indian Wells Lane north, bear left on circular drive to the resort; www.grandchampions.hyatt.com.

Marriott Desert Springs Resort
74-855 Country Club Dr, Palm Desert
Tennis club: 760/341-1893

You don't have to be Andre Agassi or Martina Hingis to play here at one of **Tennis** *magazine's 50 Greatest Resorts in the United States: This resort has 3 clay, 2 grass, and 15 hard courts, with 6 courts lighted for night play. Hourly rates for the public during peak season are $22 for hard courts, $27 for clay, and $32 for grass. Hotel guests get priority; it's easier for nonguests to get a court during the summer, when rates are also lower. Other services include private or semiprivate lessons, group clinics, racquet re-stringing, and a player-matching service for resort guests. Local residents can put their names on a list for matching with hotel guests as needed. The Marriott also has special tennis packages such as the one that includes a room, one hour with the ball machine, an hour-long group clinic, half-hour private lesson, and unlimited court use. Price varies according to the time of year. Take Highway 10 to Cook Street south to Country Club Drive, then west to the resort; www.marriotthotels.com/CTDCA/.*

The Racquet Club of Palm Springs
2743 N Indian Canyon Dr, Palm Springs
760/325-1281 or 800/367-0946

Spencer Tracy played at this historic hotel, as did Erroll Flynn and a host of other Hollywood characters. The club has a dozen courts available for public play (eight of them lighted); rates are about $12 per hour for day play, $20 per hour at night. The pro shop has all the usual tennis supplies, with hats and other sportswear imprinted with the club logo. Take Highway 111 to Racquet Club Drive east to Indian Canyon Drive; www.racquetclubps.com.

Palm Desert Resort Country Club
77-333 Country Club Dr, Palm Desert
760/345-2791

Although this is a private club, nonmembers can play for a fee at one of 13 courts (all lighted for night use). Ball machine rental, private lessons, and equipment rentals are also available. Rates vary widely according to the time of year; call for information. Take Highway 10 to Ramon Road, west to Bob Hope Drive, south to Country Club Drive, east to the resort; www.pdrcc.com.

DeMuth Park
4375 Mesquite Ave, Palm Springs
760/323-8272

Four tennis courts, free to the public. Take Highway 111 to Ramon Road, east to Gene Autry Drive, south to Mesquite Avenue, and turn right.

Ruth Hardy Park
Tamarisk Rd and Avenida Caballeros, Palm Springs

Eight tennis courts, seven of them lighted, free to the public. From Highway 111 take Tamarisk Road east to Avenida Caballeros and go north.

College of the Desert
43-500 Monterey Ave, Palm Desert
760/341-2491

Six tennis courts, free to the public when not in use by the college. Take Highway 111 to Fred Waring Drive, east to Monterey Avenue, and go north to the college campus.

Hayworth offers a kitchen, fireplace, and pretty French doors. The grounds are lovely, with enormous palms, broad lawns, hedges, and a genteel country-club feel. If you're coming especially for a tennis weekend, management suggests you call ahead; occasionally, tournaments are scheduled and it can be difficult to get a court. *2743 N Indian Canyon Dr; 760/325-1281 or 800/367-0946; $$; AE, DC, DIS, MC, V; no checks; www.racquetclubps.com; racquetclubps@ yahoo.com; take N Palm Canyon Dr to Racquet Club Rd east to Indian Canyon Dr and go north.*

SAN MARINO HOTEL ★★

A delightful little hotel designed by William Cody in 1947 as an homage to Frank Lloyd Wright, the San Marino offers just 16 guest rooms built around a pool. Located in the Tennis District, just a block from Palm Canyon Drive, this is a peaceful, low-key place that caters to a grown-up clientele seeking a place to relax and rejuvenate. Tranquility is the watchword at this hostelry, which tends to attract faithful repeat visitors; as the resident manager says, "At the San Marino, we sell quiet." Each room has a quaint, individual look, with custom furnishings such as wrought iron or carved headboards, neatly dressed beds (topped with down comforters), and original art on the walls. Some include full kitchens, as well as private patios or balconies, and the second-story rooms in particular have terrific mountain views. Poolside, visitors are welcome to use the barbecue and set up alfresco meals. One ground-floor guest room has been adapted for wheelchair access. *225 W Baristo Rd; 760/325-6902 or 800/676-1214; $$; AE, MC, V; checks OK; info@san marinohotel.com; www.palmsprings.com/sanmarino; take Palm Canyon Dr to Baristo Rd and go west.* ♿

SPA HOTEL & CASINO ★

This older hotel is quite popular with families, as well as health-conscious guests who come to enjoy the mineral waters. Built on the site of mineral hot springs used by the Cahuilla Indians centuries ago, the hotel has two therapeutic soaking pools, as well as a conventional swimming pool. The 230 rooms have been refurbished over the years, and are clean and comfy, if not fancy. For more spacious quarters, upgrade to a one-bedroom suite. Nonsmoking and handicapped-accessible lodgings are available by request. It's the on-site casino and the spa facilities (which have been remodeled and expanded) that really make the hotel worth a visit. The casino is open 24 hours, seven days a week, with a variety of live and video gambling games. At the spa, a quiet spot with muted lighting, the men's and women's facilities offer services including soothing rubdowns, specialty facials, and "inhalation therapy" in a eucalyptus-scented steam room. Whether or not you're a hotel guest, you can take advantage of the "Spa Experience," a package that includes sauna, some deep breathing in the eucalyptus inhalation room, a soak in the mineral waters in your own private tub, and quiet time in the Tranquility Room. It's $20 for hotel guests, $25 for the public. The property is owned by the Agua Caliente band of the Cahuilla tribe; the on-site museum shop features Native American music, jewelry, and crafts. *100 N Indian Canyon Dr, Palm Springs; 760/325-1461 or 800/854-1279; $$; AE, DC, DIS, MC, V; checks OK; www.hotel@aguacaliente.org; at Tahquitz Canyon Wy.* &

VILLA ROYALE ☆☆☆

Combine the suave, self-assured elegance of a classic European villa with gardens Monet would have approved of, and you get this oasis just outside the city center. Stately, peaceful, and very grown-up (children are not encouraged here, nor are they missed), Villa Royale is the place to nurture a romance, work on one's novel, or simply bask in the lavender-scented courtyards. Surrounded by walls and greenery, guest rooms range from the simple, studiolike Hideaway Guestrooms to one- and two-bedroom suites with fireplaces, kitchens, living rooms, and patio. Some offer private hot tubs as well. All are decorated in typical European style, featuring lofty down comforters, soothing colors, and themes ranging from French country cottage to Tuscan retreat. Two pools (open 24 hours) and a large Jacuzzi are available for soaking away one's cares, although the ambience here should have you plenty relaxed within your first five minutes. The inn's restaurant, Europa, is a favorite destination of in-the-know diners throughout the desert. Not only is it inviting, with a sunset color scheme, three fireplaces, and neatly dressed tables, Europa is serious about French and Mediterranean cuisine. Signature dishes are well-prepared versions of filet mignon, pan-roasted duck, rack of lamb, and salmon cooked in parchment. For dessert, either tarte Tatin or crème brûlée do nicely. In addition to the main dining room, a smaller private area may be reserved in advance. Room rates include a custom-cooked breakfast each day. *1620 Indian Trail, Palm Springs; 760/327-2314 or 800/245-2314; $$$; AE, DIS, DC, MC, V; checks OK; www.villaroyale.com; take E Palm Canyon Dr to Indian Trail and go north.*

THE WILLOWS HISTORIC
PALM SPRINGS INN   ★★★★

Everything glorious about Palm Springs's past—its history as a glamorous getaway, intellectual haven, nature sanctuary, and rejuvenative spa—lives on at the Willows. The eight-room inn was built in 1927 as a private estate. New York attorney and multimillionaire Samuel Untermyer bought it soon thereafter and massaged it into elegant perfection. Today the house steps up a hillside above old Palm Springs, its Tuscan-yellow walls, red-tile roofs, and multiple terraces tangoing in and out of a grove of tall palms, fringed willows, and the stone mountainside itself. Owners Tracy Conrad and Paul Marut, both emergency-room doctors with a penchant for architectural triage, purchased the house in 1994. According to Conrad, it was but a forlorn husk of its days when Albert Einstein spent weeks visiting Untermyer, when Clark Gable and Carole Lombard hid away for a honeymoon, and when, in the 1950s, Marion Davies, mistress of William Randolph Hearst, owned it and converted the only kitchen to a bar. Today every surface and every furnishing has been restored, from door hinges to flagstones. Rooms are large and tastefully furnished with fine antiques. Each terrace reveals a view of gardens and the ragged curtain of mountains beyond. A 50-foot waterfall burbles down the mountainside into the breakfast patio. The inn's full-time staff serves a glorious breakfast (the bread pudding with walnut and berry sauce is heaven, accompanied by scrambled eggs with chèvre and chives) and keeps the service intuitively unintrusive without being stuffy. No outside visitors roam the grounds (although many ask). At twilight, as the desert cools, guests gather in an open veranda room beneath a Moroccan-arched ceiling to sip wine and enjoy hors d'oeuvres. At bedtime (after a day of swimming and reading), the crisp cotton sheets welcome your tanned skin, and the open terrace doors to your room admit the hushed twitters of birds settling in for a night in the palms. As are you. *412 W Tahquitz Canyon Wy, Palm Springs; 760/320-0771; $$$$; AE, DC, DIS, MC, V; checks OK; www.thewillowspalmsprings.com; 2 blocks toward mountains off Palm Canyon Dr, across from Le Vallauris.*

CATHEDRAL CITY, RANCHO MIRAGE, AND PALM DESERT

CATHEDRAL CITY

Often overlooked by visitors "just driving through" from Palm Springs, Cathedral City is bordered by Highway 111 to the west and south and Interstate 10 to the north. Currently expanding thanks to some major redevelopment projects, the town is home to a growing number of families and has a year-round population of about 36,000. It's also the site of the College of the Desert, a community college known not only for education but also for its open-air market each weekend.

You won't see any grandiose cathedrals, however. According to the Chamber of Commerce, the region got its name in 1850, when a member of the U.S. Army Corps of Engineers decided that the local canyons resembled the cavernous interiors of grand churches. Hence the name Cathedral Canyon, followed in the 1920s by developers who dubbed a subdivision Cathedral City.

At the heart of the city's redevelopment is the new complex along Highway 111 that holds the city's civic center, police department, Mary Pickford Theater (a movie theater and restaurant complex), and IMAX theater.

For more information about the community, contact the Cathedral City Chamber of Commerce (760/328-1213; www.cathedralcitycc.com).

ACTIVITIES

 Experience IMAX. The new IMAX Desert Theater (68-510 E Palm Canyon Dr; 760/324-7333 or 888/340-2460) draws fans from Palm Springs to Indio, since it's the only theater of its kind in the Coachella Valley. It's also one of the select theaters in the IMAX family to offer 3D films as well as conventional 2D movies on topics such as nature, the wilderness, travel, and superstar Michael Jordan. The stunning cinematography, six-story-high screen, and awesome sound system make this a fun, memorable diversion for kids and adults alike. Seating is assigned, a nice touch when attendance is high. And here's a tip: No matter how searing the sun, the IMAX theater is always cool; some regulars joke that they come here no matter what's playing, just to get cooled off. Tickets are available at the theater or by phone. (Open every day; adults, $7.75, kids, $5.75; info@desert

The Fountain of Life, unveiled in Cathedral City's Town Square near the IMAX in July 2000, is a stone structure designed to be an interactive sculpture for kids and adults. Honoring the wildlife and history of the desert, the Fountain of Life combines water features, sculptures, and a soft-rubber-floor surface so little ones don't skin their knees.

imax.com; www.desertimax.com; E Palm Canyon Dr at Cathedral Canyon Dr.)

Big League Dreams Sports Park. Here in the heart of the desert lies a real-life field of dreams, with softball fields created as replicas of Chicago's Wrigley Field, New York's Yankee Stadium, and Boston's Fenway Park. Leagues made up of desert residents are the most frequent players on the fields here (five in total), but the complex also hosts exhibitions, baseball fantasy camps (where wanna-be jocks can play with their major league heroes), and tournaments. Softball is the main attraction, supplemented by other activities such as volleyball and basketball, batting cages and soccer fields. The park is also available for private parties and corporate gatherings by advance reservation. The public is welcome to drop by and have a look around or use the batting cage; there's a $1.50 admission fee (33-700 Date Palm Dr; 760/324-5600 or 888/390-7275; www.bigleaguedreams .com; take E Palm Canyon Dr to Date Palm Dr and go north).

Camelot Park Family Entertainment Center. Custom-made for kids, this amusement park has modern video games, laser tag, and a motion simulator ride. Happily, it also offers the old-fashioned stuff that appeals to the kid in all of us: miniature golf, go-karts, a batting cage, arcade games, and bumper boats. Open every day, year-round: Monday to Thursday 11am to 10pm; Friday 11am to midnight; Saturday 10am to midnight; Sunday 10am to 10pm. Admission is free; pay per activity. Family fun-packs are available. (67-700 E Palm Canyon Dr, Cathedral City; 760/321-9893.)

Bowling. With 28 lanes, the newly remodeled Palm Springs Lanes (68-051 Ramon Rd; 760/324-8204) welcomes bowlers seven days a week. These popular lanes are home to league members, occasional players, and beginners. You don't even have to keep score; machines do it for you automatically. It's a far cry from the days of pinsetters and score cards. Open until midnight on some days of the week; call in advance to check.

 Rest in peace. Several prominent entertainers are buried at Desert Memorial Park (69-920 E Ramon Rd), including

Frank Sinatra, whose headstone reads "The Best Is Yet to Come." Other celebs include composer Frederick Loewe; producer Busby Berkeley; former Palm Springs mayor, congressman, and singer Sonny Bono; and *Thin Man* actor William Powell. (From E Palm Canyon Dr/Hwy 111 in Cathedral City take Date Palm Dr north to Ramon Rd, then east to the cemetery near Da Vall Dr.)

RESTAURANTS

EL GALLITO ★★

Don't let the shabby exterior, dusty parking lot, and bars on the front windows deter you. Everybody in the valley goes to this little Mexican restaurant—at least, everyone who loves cheap, abundant, consistently good food. El Gallito is the kind of place where the glasses are plastic and the carpet is faded, but nobody cares because they're scarfing down massive pork tamales and shredded beef tacos; jumbo-sized combo plates and perfectly fried chile rellenos. The crowd ranges from local families and regulars, many of them Hispanic, to tourists lucky enough to have heard about the place. The setting is ultracasual and it's generally packed with people filling the red Naugahyde booths or awaiting a take-out order by the cash register. A few house rules apply and are listed on the menu or on various signs: cash only; three drink maximum (beer and wine only are served); no shirt, no shoes, no service. We especially like the posting that announces, "If you have reservations, you're in the wrong place." *68-820 Grove St, Cathedral City; 760/328-7794; $; cash only; lunch, dinner every day; beer and wine; no reservations; just north of Hwy 111 near intersection of Van Fleet St.*

RANCHO MIRAGE

Eleven miles from Palm Springs, quiet Rancho Mirage is perhaps best known to outsiders as the home of the Betty Ford Center (39-000 Bob Hope Dr), as well as former presidents Gerald Ford and Dwight Eisenhower.

But this wealthy, low-profile town is also the site of several high-profile professional golf tournaments, and perhaps some

Road sign you're least likely to see back home: "Caution: Bighorn Sheep," along Highway 111 in Rancho Mirage.

celebrity remains. Rumor has it that after Harpo Marx was cremated, his ashes were scattered into a sand trap at the seventh hole of the Rancho Mirage golf course.

These days, everyone's talking about the enormous complex being built on Highway 111 and scheduled to open by September 2001. Known as the River, the shopping and entertainment center has already signed Borders Books and Music, Edwards Cinemas, and Prego Italian restaurant as tenants. People are abuzz, too, about the new casino at the corner of Bob Hope Drive and Ramon Road; some see it as a pot of gold filled with jobs and recreation, others as a Pandora's box of traffic, light pollution, and noise.

For more information about the community, contact the Rancho Mirage Chamber of Commerce (42-464 Rancho Mirage Ln; 760/568-9351; www.ranchomirage.org).

ACTIVITIES

Children's Discovery Museum of the Desert. Serious fun: That's what this marvelous museum built especially for kids is all about. With more than 50 exhibits, many of them interactive, there's something here to entertain toddlers as well as grade-school-aged kids. But it's not just about entertainment. The facility's stated goal is to inspire and challenge young minds in a supportive, lighthearted environment. Wonderfully messy art projects, archaeological "digs," ballet classes, gardening demonstrations, storytelling, you name it—this place knows how to show young people a great time while helping them to learn. Parents or guardians are asked to stay with their kids throughout their visits here—not so much to supervise, as to help them explore and enjoy the many experiences here. In addition to its regular programs and exhibits, the museum hosts field trips, programs for toddlers, day camps, parties, and workshops. Open Tuesday to Saturday 10am to 5pm; Sunday noon to 5pm; also Mondays from January to April 10am to 5pm. Admission is $5 per person aged 2 and over; free for kids 1 or younger. Note: Museum membership is $15 per person annually and allows unlimited entry to the museum as well as a 10 percent discount in the museum store. (71-701 Gerald Ford Dr; 760/321-0602; www.cdmod.org.)

GOLF CART PARADE

As befits a community where a household's second car is often a golf cart, the annual parade starring the carts moonlighting as Rose Parade floats is a big deal. Started in 1964 as a bit of a joke, the parade has grown to a well-publicized event attracting an estimated 25,000 spectators and more than 100 whimsically transformed carts. Past parades have seen giant slot machines, outsized golf bags, a spectacular Noah's Ark, and a champagne bottle all motoring majestically up one side of El Paseo and down the other. Held each November, the parade is free. 760/346-6111; www.golfcartparade.com.

Nabisco Championship Golf Tournament. The top women in golf compete at this annual event, one of four major championships on the LPGA circuit. Formerly known as the Dinah Shore Golf Classic, the tournament is especially popular with lesbians, who come to watch top-notch golf during the day and attend a round of pool parties, dances, comedy shows, and concerts sponsored by various organizations every night. The tournament is held every March at the Mission Hills Country Club on Dinah Shore Drive. Tournament tickets are available at the gate, on-line, or by phone (760/324-4546 or www.nabiscochampionship.com).

Bob Hope Chrysler Classic. Founded in 1960, this tournament attracts the top male players in the world, as well as celebs like Bill Murray, Alice Cooper, Michael Jordan, Vince Gill, and Leslie Nielsen. Over the years, it's raised more than $33 million for a number of local charities, and made history in 1995 when Presidents Bill Clinton, George Bush, and Gerald Ford joined Bob Hope for the tournament's opening round. The week-long event is held on four different courses in the area. Headquarters are at 39-000 Bob Hope Drive in Rancho Mirage; buy tickets there, on-line, or by phone (760/346-8184 or 888/672-4673; www.bhcc.com).

LODGINGS

RANCHO LAS PALMAS MARRIOTT
RESORT & SPA ★★

Desert resorts often weave golf holes close to their wings of rooms, but few do it as boldly as Rancho Las Palmas. Here 2 of the 27 Ted Robinson, Sr.–designed holes plunge right into the very center of the resort compound, water hazards and all, their greens almost at the feet of diners or sunbathers. Rancho Las Palmas's main lobby, restaurant, and conference buildings, as well as its 450 low-rise rooms and 22 suites, are comfortably spaced across a wide area. Nothing feels crowded here. Appealing tile roofs give everything a hacienda feeling, and hundreds of lanky palm trees dot the grounds. A 25-court tennis club, as well as several pools and Tortuga Island, a 6,000-square-foot water playground with slide and pop jets for family fun, complete the sporting scene. More languid luxury is offered at the 20,000-square-foot European-style health spa, which features 26 treatment rooms, saunas, steam, hydrotherapy, two fitness centers, and an outdoor pool with underwater music. While activity is generally geared toward the out-of-doors, the recently remodeled and refurbished rooms, with French doors opening onto private balconies, television armoires, and Mission-style furnishings, provide a serene setting for moments of rest. Mediterranean-style fine dining is featured each evening at Madeira, while Pablo's Restaurant and Tapas Bar is open all day, serving American food as well as Spanish specialties. In the hotel spa, Fresca's offers light, guilt-free cuisine. Alas, like several other large resorts built out on the flat desert plain in the Coachella Valley, Rancho Las Palmas turns inward and doesn't offer a great sense of place: It's just not close enough to the mountains. But it creates its own self-contained world, and families can stay here for days without feeling the need to go anywhere else. *41-000 Bob Hope Dr, Rancho Mirage; 760/568-2727 or 800/458-8786; $$$; AE, DC, DIS, MC, V; checks OK; www.marriott.com/ marriott/pspca; near corner of Hwy 111 and Bob Hope Dr.* ᬬ

RITZ-CARLTON RANCHO MIRAGE ✭✭✭✭

 The only major resort hotel in the Coachella Valley region that's actually in the spectacular mountains, the uber-luxurious Ritz-Carlton is perched high above Highway 111. In contrast to the towering mountains, the hotel's architecture is linear, modern, and horizontal—a broad U open to the view. A bronze statue of a bighorn sheep greets you in the porte cochere, but inside all evidence of the desert's natural world vanishes; you're in a French country palace with marble floors, French antiques, baroque paintings, and long halls. The elegant guest rooms (240 of them, arranged in three-story wings) all have private balconies with views of the pool, mountains, or valley—or all three. Accommodations are spacious, with elegant stone finishes, luxurious fabrics, and crisp linens. A "club" floor offers added amenities: a private lounge, personal concierge, and complimentary food and beverage service during the day. The Ritz's swimming pool is one of the best in the desert: Viewed from the hotel's main balcony, it looks like a David Hockney painting lined with blue and white cabanas near a canyon edge. Tennis players are well served at the Ritz, with 10 hard courts and 1 clay court to choose from. No public play: You must be a guest to enjoy the courts here. Croquet is also available on a permanent grass court on the east side. The on-site fitness and beauty spa offers over 30 different treatments. Or if it's a simple soak you want, the outdoor hydro-spa has the best view in the valley: It perches on the very rim of the hotel property. The hotel's restaurants are often booked solid, not only because of their excellence but also due to a tendency for guests to "stay in" rather than roam the tawdry valley below. The Mirada, an ultracasual poolside dining area, features light items such as salads, appetizers, soups, and pastas (as well as frosty cocktails just perfect for sipping on a chaise lounge). It generally closes by 6pm. The Cafe offers California cuisine, and the Dining Room, which is closed June through October, elegantly explores French/Mediterranean. Service at the Ritz can be particularly formal but is always first-rate. *68-900 Frank Sinatra Dr, Rancho Mirage; 760/321-8282 or 800/241-3333; $$$$; AE, DC, DIS, MC, V; checks OK; www.ritz carlton.com; from I-10, take Date Palm Dr south to Hwy 111, go left to Frank Sinatra Dr, then right.* ♿

Of the valley's many resorts built in the 1980s and 1990s in the flat desert neighborhoods north of Highway 111, the Westin ranks at the top for artful elegance without glitz. Its architecture recalls a Moroccan palace, so it seems to fit the desert clime perfectly. Long, open arcades stretch in several directions from the central shopping and lobby plaza. Sounds of splashing children draw you toward an oasis-like pool where a 60-foot water slide springs from a minimountain (two other pools indulge adults only). Surrounded by the Mission Hills Country Club courses, one designed by Pete Dye and the other by Gary Player, the Westin caters to serious golfers and tennis players, but also gives the read-a-book guest quiet balconies and restful rooms. (A unique angled arrangement of the large, comfortable beds lets you gaze out the window at distant mountains.) Two restaurants celebrate indoor-outdoor dining during the high season when cooler winter temperatures prevail: Bella Vista (California cuisine) and La Concha (contemporary American). Children under 18 stay free, and numerous camp-like programs and babysitters keep them busy. Service here can be exceptionally friendly, and the clientele seems more relaxed than at many other resorts closer to in-town nightlife. *71-333 Dinah Shore Dr, Rancho Mirage; 760/328-5955 or 800/937-8461; $$$$; AE, DC, DIS, MC, V; no checks; ranch@westin.com; www.westin.com; at Bob Hope Dr.* &

PALM DESERT

Shoppers, take heart: you've found the equivalent of Beverly Hills's Rodeo Drive transplanted to the desert. Palm Desert's El Paseo boasts almost a hundred boutiques, gift and antique shops, and galleries, as well as a number of worthwhile restaurants. Simply walking up one side of the divided street and down the other gives you about a mile of nonstop window-shopping and browsing. The people-watching isn't half bad, either: trophy wives (and husbands), realtors with a cell phone in each hand, tourists with outrageous sunburns, svelte senior citizens in tennis garb, babies dressed up like fancy sugarplums.

While you're wandering this street of dreams, be sure to check out the Gardens on El Paseo (73-585 El Paseo at Larkspur). The entrance to this aptly named, two-level mall boasts a gorgeous desert garden accented with paths, sculpture, fountains, and native plants. Beyond the garden area a Saks Fifth Avenue awaits, along with lots of exclusive shops and trendy restaurants.

Across Highway 111 is the Westfield Shopping Town Palm Desert (72-840 Hwy 111; 760/776-6560), formerly known as Palm Desert Town Center, which is jam-packed with stores, boutiques, fast-food arcades, and even an ice-skating rink.

For more information about the community, contact the Palm Desert Visitor Information Center (72-990 Hwy 111, at the corner of Hwy 111 and Monterey Ave; 760/568-1441 or 800/873-2428; www.palm-desert.org).

ACTIVITIES

Visit a wild kingdom. The Living Desert Wildlife and Botanical Park (47-900 Portola Ave; 760/346-5694; www.livingdesert.org) is a fascinating place to spend a few hours viewing desert wildlife and plants. Established in 1970 as a nonprofit education and conservation center, the Living Desert is home to more than 400 animals: native bighorn sheep, mountain lions, eagles, and kit foxes as well as imported exotics such as cheetahs, zebras, meerkats, and Arabian oryx. Much more than just a zoo, the park offers a look at the ecology of various desert regions throughout the world, and illustrates how plants and animals have adapted to these arid, often harsh environments. It's suitable for visitors of all ages, with hiking trails, botanical gardens, aviaries, and places to simply sit and observe.

The newest attraction, Village WaTuTu, is a replica of a northeast African village, with mud-walled huts and thatched roofs. Here, animals include leopards, camels, and hyenas, and there's a petting zoo for kids. The Living Desert also has a captive breeding program aimed at encouraging endangered species to reproduce and avoid extinction. To reach the park from Highway 111 in Palm Desert, turn south on Portola Avenue, go 1.5 miles, and follow signs to main entrance. Open every day 9am to 5pm; reduced hours during summer, 8am to 1:30pm. Admission is $8.50 for adults, $4.25 for kids; discounts for seniors and groups.

Native plants are all the rage in Southwest gardens. Pick up some cacti, yuccas, or other hardy desert natives at the Palo Verde Garden Center, which is part of the Living Desert Wildlife and Botanical Park. The center also has several exhibition gardens to provide inspiration and guidance before you start digging holes in your yard.

CONSIGNMENT SHOPPING

Along with showcasing some of the heavy hitters of the fashion world—Prada, Escada, St. John, Chanel—Palm Desert is big on high-end consignment shops. These are stores that buy and sell the cast-off furnishings of the famous and the well-to-do, many of whom redecorate every couple of seasons.

No plaid loveseats or Naugahyde recliners here. At these stores the merchandise tends to be genuine Gallé glassware from France, intricately inlaid Chinese chests, dazzling one-of-a-kind lead crystal chandeliers, and custom-made living room and bedroom sets.

At the Classic Consignment Company (73-847 El Paseo, Palm Desert; 760/568-4948), price tags in the mid-to-high five figures aren't unusual. Many of the shop's consigners are wealthy antique collectors who buy top-quality period furniture in Europe, then turn around and sell it a few years later when they change their decor. Others are celebrities; Kay Ballard and Shecky Green are among the famous faces who have used the shop to sell items.

The shop's John Dew says certain consigners with splendid taste and quality goods practically inspire fan clubs among consumers and interior designers. "For awhile our price tags had the name of the consigners on them," Dew explained. "One lady had some very special designer items and she became a favorite with the decorators who'd call and say, 'Do you have anything from Mrs. So and So in?' She was a wonderful woman with very good taste."

Dew adds that even for the wealthy, consignment shopping is a matter of paying the lowest price for the best merchandise. "We might have a chair for $995, and down the street it's $1,650. The person who buys our chair will go out and buy a Louis Vuitton handbag with what she saves."

Shoppers on a tighter budget can also find plenty of lower priced items, even in the priciest consignment stores in Palm Desert and the other desert cities. Look for vintage costume jewelry; barware and crystal from Lalique and Waterford; and prints, small paintings and photographs, lamps, and other smaller items; some are under $100. If you're interested in a particular genre or period, you can ask storekeepers to keep *you posted when finds come in. And don't be afraid to ask for a better deal. Often, the dealers have room to negotiate prices. Some other recommended shops include:*

The Estate Sale Company (4185 E Palm Canyon Dr, Palm Springs; 760/321-7628) is across the highway from Merv Griffin's Resort Hotel and Givenchy Spa. Slightly worn furniture, from antique to modern, and estate jewelry are an especially good bet. The art gallery in the rear has a well-priced selection of contemporary art, including celebrity photos, oil and acrylic paintings, and limited edition prints. Next door, check out Patsy's, home to lots of gently used designer wear and cast-off celebrity treasures.

Angel View Thrift Shops, which benefit charity, not consigners, can be found throughout the valley. Look for the "Prestige Boutiques," which carry designer label and custom-made clothing, sometimes never worn (you'll find one of these at 886 N Palm Canyon Rd, Palm Springs; 760/327-0644). The shops also offer some brand-new clothing, with the labels removed, that's been donated by stores and manufacturers. Their tax write-off could be your new treasure.

From "Felix the Cat" memorabilia to '50s dinettes to massive armoires, the kicky Village Emporium (849 N Palm Canyon Dr; 760/320-6165) offers up a dizzying selection of lighthearted kitsch and high-quality home furnishings. The place is vast, so allot yourself plenty of time to wander the aisles while you talk yourself into buying a giant martini set or some movie star memorabilia.

Skate park. Both skateboarders and in-line skaters are welcome at this 15,000-square-foot facility, which is open year-round from 6am to 10pm and is lighted for night use. The park charges $5 per person for a skate card, which is good for unlimited visits for a year. All ages are allowed, but anyone under 14 needs parental or guardian consent. The park, one of the few in the desert area, can get pretty crowded, so watch out for novices. The rules require use of a helmet and elbow, wrist, and knee pads; you'll need to bring your own (Palm Desert Civic Center Park, 43-900 San Pablo Ave; take Hwy 111 to Fred Waring Dr east to San Pablo Ave and go north; 760/568-9697).

Bicycling is a leisurely way to take in the El Paseo sights and shops without worrying about a parking place. Mac's Bicycle Rental (44-841 San Pablo Ave; 760/321-9444) is open year-round and offers hourly, daily, and weekly rates on bikes, including kids' and mountain models.

Imago Galleries. Palm Desert abounds with art galleries, but this contemporary new space is one of our favorites. Specializing in art glass and sculpture, the gallery includes a library and adjacent sculpture garden. Noted glass artist Dale Chihuly, whose work includes the riot of blown glass flowers above the lobby of Las Vegas's Bellagio hotel, is one of the featured exhibitors here. So are notables like Italo Scanga and Fernando Botero (45-450 Hwy 74, 1 block south of El Paseo; 760/776-989).

McCallum Theater for the Performing Arts. This local treasure has an international scope: Audiences can applaud the Paul Taylor Dance Company one night; Kathleen Battle, Branford Marsalis, or Rita Rudner the next. Tickets are available singly or by subscription, with single-ticket prices averaging around $40. The theater is in the Bob Hope Cultural Center on the campus of College of the Desert (73-000 Fred Waring Dr; 760/346-6505; mccallum.theater.org).

Weekend street fair. Bargains in pricey Palm Desert? Absolutely—just drop by the weekly street fair held Saturday and Sunday at College of the Desert. This you-name-it, they've-got-it affair has a farmers market as well as an impressive selection of new and used clothing, real and alleged antiques, paintings, crafts, and just plain junk. Best buys include designer sunglasses (or at least, creditable knockoffs), handbags, handcrafted jewelry, and fresh produce. Parking and admission are free; hours are 7am to 2pm (they close at noon during the summer). Take Highway 111 to Fred Waring Drive and go east to the College of the Desert; the fair sets up in parking lots 9, 11, 12, 12T, and 16 off Fred Waring Drive.

Look to the stars. Sky Watcher Star Gazing Tours are for anyone who's ever longed to see the moons of Jupiter and the rings of Saturn, or wondered how to tell Antares from Vega. Proprietor Craig Herkimer and his staff use high-powered telescopes, computer guidance systems, binoculars, and good old-fashioned storytelling to explain various constellations, planets, satellites, and galaxies. Guests get lessons not only in finding and identifying objects in the night sky, but also in the mythology, astronomy, and folklore surrounding them. Free programs are offered weekly at some desert resorts (for example, the Miramonte in Indian Wells hosts a program every Friday at 8:30pm), but Sky Watcher also hosts private viewing parties for groups of any size. Programs can range from two to three hours long. For information on private parties, or the names of hotels hosting free programs, contact Sky Watcher (44-489 Town Center Wy, Suite D; 760/345-2363 or 877/3-METEOR; www.sky-watcher.com).

Desert Holocaust Memorial. In solemn contrast to the desert's general air of tranquility and *joie de vivre*, this memorial reminds visitors of a horror that occurred little more than 50 years ago. The heart of the memorial features seven bronze figures representing the spirit and suffering of the people who lived, and died, during the Holocaust. Faces and images on the memorial were inspired by photographs and news footage at the United States Holocaust Museum in Washington, D.C. Free. At Palm Desert Civic Center Park, San Pablo Avenue and Fred Waring Drive.

Every summer, Palm Desert hosts a free Summer of Fun Concert and Movie series on Thursday nights. Visitors are encouraged to bring picnics, as well as blankets, flash-lights, and lawn chairs. Musical pro-grams and family-appropriate movies alternate weeks; both start at 7:30pm at Palm Desert Civic Center Park, San Pablo Avenue at Fred Waring Drive; 760/346-6111.

RESTAURANTS

THE DAILY GRILL ★

Heaps of hot, salty shoestring fries obscure your superb bacon, lettuce, and tomato sandwich. Sips from a rich, amber pint of cold Anchor Steam beer chill your desert-parched throat. You could be in San Francisco, but you're not. Soon you'll step back outside into the unmistakable heat of the low desert, but for now you and other diners in the busy lunchtime crowd are ensconced within mahogany walls and served by a white-aproned wait staff. That's the plus side of the Daily Grill. And the minus side? That very same sense of tradition: The Grill's formula has been transplanted to Palm Desert by marketing types who've also opened several other branches around the Southland. It feels slick and planned. Yet though such formulaic restaurants never give you a sense of spontaneity, they can still offer up a good meal. Dinners range from large, savory char-broiled burgers, chicken pot pies, and broiled half chickens to more complex dishes such as chicken Marsala or broiled shrimp pomodoro with angel hair pasta. Although the place isn't open for breakfast, an early lunch here offers breakfast items such as Joe's Special (egg, spinach, onion, and hamburger scramble), eggs Benedict, bacon and eggs, and an omelet filled with Cobb ingredients. *73-061 El Paseo, Palm Desert; 760/779-9911; $; AE, DC, DIS, MC, V; no checks; lunch, dinner every day, brunch Sun; full bar; reservations not necessary; www.dailygrill.com; from Hwy 111, turn south on Monterey Ave and drive 1 block.* &

JILLIAN'S ★★★

Beauty without pretension makes Jillian's a real find amidst desert resort bistros that cater to the well-heeled crowd. The decor here is elegantly rustic, with cottage-y dining rooms, doors, windows, and porches that open up to a magical center court where palms lit with twinkle lights seem like pillars holding up the night sky. Proprietors Jay and June Trubee are well known in the desert for starting Cunard's in La Quinta (now the La Quinta Grill) in 1986 for the Cunard family. They moved on to open Jillian's in 1994, and to this day Jay does the honors in the kitchen. He trained at the Culinary Institute in Hyde Park, and his style is robust Americana, but with a strong emphasis on homemade pastas. All are made fresh daily and include such favorites as cannelloni—delicate tubes filled with four imported cheeses and served with a tomato-tinted cream sauce. Rack of lamb is another tour de force: a Colorado rack crusted with seasoned breadcrumbs and served with a demi-glace scented with homegrown rosemary. Whitefish dijonnaise arrives on a bed of mashed potatoes beneath a Pomeray-mustard hollandaise. Desserts are made on the premises (as are all breads). Jay's Hawaiian cheesecake has been featured in *Gourmet* magazine; its macadamia nut crust provides a little crunch beneath a creamy filling, pineapple topping, and fresh raspberry sauce. *74-155 El Paseo, Palm Desert; 760/776-8242; $$$ AE, DC, MC, V; local checks only; dinner every day in season, closed Jun–early Oct; full bar; reservations recommended; jillians@local.net; near Larrea St.* &

JOVANNA'S ★★★

Jovanna Cruz is everywhere: in the kitchen, at the front door, on the outdoor dining porch, in the back room. In her small, narrow restaurant—very much like a New York Italian eatery, where space is so tight the wait staff brush past each other back to back—Jovanna fills the space like the outgoing, hearty Philadelphian she is. She earned her chef's stripes at her parents' 1,800-meal-a-night restaurant in Acapulco, often putting in 18-hour days. Her pasta dishes are delicious, generous mountains of flavor, especially a combo of sautéed chicken tenders in a creamy basil sauce topped with bay shrimp and served over a bed of pasta. Osso buco is often on the menu, as is a pan-seared pork loin and a signature side dish, crispy fried spinach. Cap your meal with one of her seasonal crème brûlées: eggnog during the holidays, orange liqueur in spring, toasted coconut in summer, pumpkin in fall. *74-063 Hwy 111, Palm Desert; 760/568-1315; $$; AE, MC, V; no checks; dinner Wed–Sun (Wed–Sat in Aug); full bar; reservations recommended; near Portola Ave on the south side of Hwy 111.* &

KEEDY'S FOUNTAIN & GRILL ★

Also known as "Keedy's Fix," this classic cafe and its burgers haven't changed an iota since Bob Keedy established the joint in 1957. It's changed ownership a few times since then, but still delivers the goods. You know the menu: classic American breakfast and lunch standards like omelets, BLTs, burgers, and patty melts. But a little bit of Mexico sneaks in. Try a menudo and tortillas special, spicy carne asada, or any of the classic enchilada-taco combos. Breakfast boasts more than a bit of Mex, too, with huevos rancheros, chorizo and eggs, and machaca (shredded beef and eggs). The heart-attack classic is still great: a triple-decker burger with bacon, along with a milk shake from the fountain. On your way out, take some time to look over the magazine photo collages on the wall. Americana—you gotta love it. *73-633 Hwy 111, Palm Desert; 760/346-6492; $; AE, DIS, MC, V; no checks; breakfast, lunch every day; no alcohol; reservations not accepted; just off the south side of Hwy 111.* &

The coolest place to hear live jazz in Palm Desert is Sullivan's Steakhouse, where a talented combo jams most nights in the bar. The restaurant, home to a good-looking, martini-drinking crowd, is upstairs in the Gardens in the El Paseo complex; 73-505 El Paseo, Palm Desert; 760/341-3560.

NATIVE FOODS   ★★

Native Foods feeds on the energy of co-owner Tanya Petrovna and her passion for vegetarian cooking with an international slant. The Bali Burger may sound like just another veggie patty, but Tanya makes it from scratch, then enlivens it with caramelized onions and guacamole (you can also order it blackened, Cajun style). Big salads come out of the kitchen like baskets full of produce from a garden. Most unusual is the Jamaican Jerk Steak salad, a seitan "steak" (a vegetarian alternative to meat) over jasmine rice and romaine with flamed banana salsa. Tacos are another specialty, and they've gained fame among locals whose visiting friends are convinced that the tasty soy-based filling must be ground beef. Dinner entrees are hearty and require a few more trenching tools than ten fingers: Try the baked yam topped with steamed vegetables, or I Love Lucy's Lasagna, whose pasta layers alternate with squash, tofu, roasted eggplant and peppers, garlic cloves, and spinach. Decor is much fun as the food: Giant African-motif masks cover the walls. The crowd is hip, healthy, and every age from toddling to tottering. For dessert, tofu-based creamy dressing over carrot cake gets its zest from oranges, and Elephant's Revenge combines chocolate, coconut, and peanut butter in a rich, cinnamon-spiced cake. There is a second location in Palm Springs. *73-890 El Paseo, Palm Desert; 760/836-9396; 1775 E Palm Canyon Dr, Palm Springs; 760/416-0070; $; no credit cards; checks OK; lunch, dinner Mon–Sat; no alcohol; reservations not accepted; www.palmsprings.com/health/ nativefoods; a few steps off El Paseo near San Luis Rey Ave.* &

RUTH'S CHRIS STEAK HOUSE   ★★★

When it comes to cooking a steak, Ruth's Chris definitely has the process down. They start with corn-fed Midwestern beef, the kind so tender that you imagine it came from steers who were carried about in sedan chairs. They broil it at high heat to seal in the juices, top it with butter (talk about gilding the lily), and carry it, still sizzling, to your table. Eating here costs a small fortune, since you pay extra for side dishes and salads, but to carnivores it's worth it for what may be the best steak in the desert. For the ultimate in beefy flavor and buttery texture, get the New York strip. Filet mignons are also exceptional here, as are the whopping veal chops. Not into red meat? The menu offers chicken and live Maine lobster, but this is definitely not a place geared toward vegetarians—unless you count the restaurant's divine chopped salad, a tumble of greens and veggies topped off with blue cheese and onion rings. Side dishes of note are the creamed spinach, the sautéed mushrooms, and the shamefully rich au gratin potatoes. As befits an old-school steak house, the surroundings are clubby, with ruddy wood paneling, white-draped tables, and gentle lighting. Service is knowledgeable and pleasant. In addition to a full bar, the restaurant is known for its pricey but extensive wine list, which highlights some top California cabernets. The place is absolutely jammed on weekends during high season, so make reservations well in advance. *74-040 Hwy 111, Palm Desert; 760/779-1998; $$$; AE, DC, DIS, MC, V; no checks; dinner every day; full bar; reservations recommended; palmdesert@ruthschris.com; www.ruthschris.com; corner of Portola Ave and Hwy 111.* &

SAMMY'S WOODFIRED PIZZA ★★

An instant hit with the pizza-loving public, Sammy's is an upscale chain that was founded in San Diego. The Palm Desert branch has a similar menu to the others, with cleverly topped pizzas cooked in wood-burning ovens the perennial bestseller. These 10-inch pies are laden with about two dozen combos from simple (mozzarella, tomatoes, and fresh basil) to elaborate (grilled shrimp, chiles, cilantro, and fresh mint). The barbecued chicken number with smoked gouda and red onions is especially fine. Good as the pizzas are, they get ample competition from Sammy's mammoth chopped salads topped with chicken or pepperoni (one of these babies will serve two or three diners) and the ambitious pasta selection. Best bets in the latter category are the now-ubiquitous chicken tequila fettucine (done quite nicely, we might add), angel hair with Italian bacon, garlic, and red peppers, and chicken pasta tossed with peanut sauce. Rotisserie chicken is the best nonpasta entree. Dessert comes in the form of simple and satisfying ice cream sundaes. The restaurant, on the second level of the Gardens of El Paseo, has the requisite misted patio as well as a capacious dining room decorated in tones of terracotta and turquoise. Reservations are only accepted for parties of six or more, so be prepared for a wait during peak hours of lunch and dinner. *73-595 El Paseo, Palm Desert; 760/836-0500; $; AE, DIS, MC, V; no checks; lunch, dinner every day; beer and wine only; no reservations; www.sammys pizza.com; El Paseo near Larkspur.*

TOMMY BAHAMA'S ★★

Carefree attitudes and Caribbean latitudes are inspired by this breezy restaurant in the tiny Gardens at El Paseo mall. Strategically located on the second floor, with a spacious balcony overlooking the street, Tommy Bahama's has a fun "let's party!" ambience that's hard to resist. The dining room and bar have a plantation-house theme, with ceiling fans, potted palms, wood tables, and servers dressed in casual island style. Outside, the patio overlooking El Paseo is sheltered by cafe umbrellas, additional greenery, and cooling misters for those days when the temperatures are equatorial. Tropical drinks are the beverage of choice, although bartenders are just as happy to whip up a martini as a mai tai, and service is swift and pleasant. As for the food, it's as appealing as the lighthearted setting. The mango shrimp salad with sweet Bermuda onions is smashing, as is the simple Caesar. For Caribbean-style grazing, get the plantain combo—conch fritters, grilled chicken skewers, coconut-crusted shrimp, and chips with salsa. Grilled salmon is a winner, either as an entree or in a sandwich; we're also partial to whatever fish of the day is offered, blackened or grilled, on a fluffy white roll. For dessert, it's got to be chocolate banana bread pudding, a combo that's wickedly good. If the decor and food get you in the mood for a little piece of the Bahamas to take home, just head downstairs to Tommy Bahama's retail store, purveyor of apparel, accessories, and other Tommy Bahamian accoutrements. *73-595 El Paseo, Palm Desert; 760/836-0188; $; AE, MC, V; no checks; lunch, dinner every day; full bar; reservations recommended for dinner; in the Gardens of El Paseo mall (El Paseo near Larkspur).*

LODGINGS

EMBASSY SUITES HOTEL ★★

Between the super-convenient location right at Highway 111 and the generously sized accommodations, the recently renovated Embassy is popular with both business and pleasure travelers. All rooms feature sleeping quarters with a king or two double beds, plus a separate living room furnished with work table and fold-out sleeper sofa. Amenities include a wet bar, microwave, fridge, and coffeemaker, as well as a TV in both the bedroom and the sitting area. For anyone more interested in play than work, the hotel has six lighted tennis courts, a pool, a gym, and an 18-hole putting green. Room rates include a simple, cooked-to-order breakfast and a complimentary happy hour each night. *74-700 Hwy 111; 760/340-6600 or 800/EMBASSY; $$; AE, DC, DIS, MC, V; checks OK; www.embassysuites.com; at Hwy 111 just west of Cook St.*

MARRIOTT'S DESERT SPRINGS RESORT AND SPA ★★★

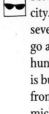 Set on 450 acres, this Marriott resembles a small, jewel-like city. With more than 900 rooms and suites spread across several wings, it's easy to get lost here, but what a place to go astray. This is one of the grandest hotels within several hundred miles. There is water, water everywhere; the resort is built on a lake and gondolas are used to transport guests from the lobby to their rooms and other destinations. Gimmicky, perhaps, but also romantic and fun. The grounds are almost Versailles-esque, with lush lawns, exuberant flower gardens, mature trees and palms, and five swimming pools. There's not much reason to leave the hotel if you don't want to, since the property has five restaurants, more than a dozen boutiques, 20 top-quality tennis courts (including grass and clay, and the staff will find you a partner if you like), two Ted Robinson, Sr.–designed golf courses, even a Jose Eber hair salon. Oh, and let's not overlook the spa. This 30,000-square-foot facility features a staggering selection of body treatments and has been named one of the top five spas in the U.S. by *Condé Nast*

Traveler. Rooms are in keeping with the rest of the hotel: spacious, each with a small balcony or patio, easy-on-the-eyes decor, and the always appreciated in-room safe, ironing board, and coffeemaker. Aaah. *74-855 Country Club Dr, Palm Desert; 760/341-2211 or 800/331-3112; $$$; AE, DC, DIS, MC, V; checks OK; www.marriott hotels.com/CTDCA/; take Hwy 111 to Country Club Dr and go east almost to Cook St.*

THOUSAND PALMS, LA QUINTA, AND INDIO

THOUSAND PALMS

With all the golf courses and houses checkerboarding the valley along Highway 111, visitors who love the natural desert are hard-pressed to find a patch of open habitat. But at Coachella Valley Preserve, you can tour 21,000 acres of relatively undisturbed "original desert." Rich in flora and fauna, the preserve has been designated a "Watchable Wildlife Site" by the California Bureau of Land Management.

The preserve is the site of several oases, where you'll find lush groves of native, shaggy-trunked Washingtonia palms—the same palms usually found deep in desert canyons. Visit the spectacular Thousand Palms Oasis and nearby McCallum Grove to view these trees, which themselves house flourishing ecosystems of spiders, snakes, rodents, and bats. The preserve also holds the last blown-sand dunes in Coachella Valley. These shifting dunes are the native habitat of the endangered fringe-toed lizard, a species unique to this area that "swims" through the fine sand on specially evolved toes to escape predators and the summer heat. The area offers excellent birding as well, with more than 180 species documented here.

The preserve is open daily from sunrise to sunset, and admission is free. To get there, take Interstate 10 east to the Ramon Road exit. Drive 5 miles north on Ramon Road; turn left on Thousand Palms Canyon Road and continue 2 miles to the visitor center; 760/343-1234.

LA QUINTA

Here's a glimpse of the old days in the Coachella Valley, but it's disappearing fast under a tide of new houses and golf courses. Still not much more than a village, La Quinta nestles in a "cove" (local parlance for a flat area of desert surrounded by mountains).

Nights are dark here: Local ordinances forbid bright lights so that residents can better enjoy the stars and the sense of living in the country. Liz Perkovich, a longtime resident, says she's seen lots of visitors come here for a getaway, fall in love with the place, and move in full time. Indeed, La Quinta is one of the fastest growing cities in the state.

The town is best known for its venerable La Quinta Resort, which opened in 1927 and has been a playground for the privileged ever since. It's also home to the acclaimed PGA West golf facility, where, at just about every hole, pros find a challenge and hackers find humility.

For more information, contact the La Quinta Chamber of Commerce (78-495 Calle Tampico; 760/564-3199; www.lq chamber.org).

THE HISTORIC LA QUINTA RESORT

Since its construction in 1926, the La Quinta Resort has been synonymous with luxury, privacy, and discretion. The property, envisioned by original owner Walter H. Morgan as a retreat for a select group of guests, began as a series of private casitas and a nine-hole golf course. Designed by architect Gordon Kaufman (who later gained fame for such projects as the Santa Anita racecourse), the hotel embodied the grace and style of classic Spanish architecture. The year after the resort opened, Morgan—a wealthy and well-connected man—invited various Hollywood celebrities to enjoy his secluded getaway. It was an instant hit with the stars, far away from fans, deadlines, pressure, and L.A. politics. Famous faces who helped put La Quinta on the society map included Ginger Rogers, Bette Davis, William Powell, Marlene Dietrich, and Clark Gable. Director Frank Capra spent time at La Quinta as well, working to adapt a short story called "Night Bus" into his classic It Happened One Night. *After the film won an Academy Award for Best Picture, it's said, Capra returned to La Quinta again and again for inspiration and good luck. The hotel closed during World War II—gas rationing made the trip from Los Angeles impossible—but re-opened after the war to more popularity than ever.*

Through the years the property changed hands and expanded several times, but the rarefied air of privilege remains. Today, La Quinta has about 640 rooms, three 18-hole golf courses, 23 tennis courts (complete with grass, clay, and hard court options), and three well-regarded restaurants. A top-notch spa offers an astonishing number of services, from good old-fashioned massage to paraffin wraps and champagne facials (honest—they use champagne yeast from France). Modern-day celebs who have stayed here range from Drew Barrymore and Candace Bergen to Jason Priestly and comedians Penn & Teller.

ACTIVITIES

La Quinta Arts Festival. Artists from throughout the country and around the world converge here each March for this high-profile, four-day art show. This is no neighborhood arts and crafts fair; the festival committee receives more than 1,000 applications each year and uses a panel of judges to narrow the entrants down to around 250. In addition to paintings in various media, the show includes sculpture, blown glass, collage, ceramics, and photographs. Prices for a single piece range anywhere from a few hundred dollars to the high five figures.

Live entertainment is a popular sideline of the event, whose honorary chairman is local resident Merv Griffin (the entertainer also hosts a variety show at the festival each year). Other diversions include daily musical performances, a wine tasting, and an abundance of food booths. Attendance over the four days averages about 30,000. Adult admission is $10 (reduced rates for children, who also are encouraged to participate in several interactive exhibits to learn more about art). The show takes place at Frances Hack Park, 77-865 Avenida Montezuma; take Highway 111 east to Washington Street south, then follow the signs. Approximate hours are 10am to 5pm Thursday and Sunday, 10am to 8pm Friday and Saturday. Note: The foundation also sponsors a number of other events, as well as classes and scholarships for children and adults. (760/564-1244; info@lqaf.com; www.lqaf.com.)

Street fair. During the winter months, the city hosts monthly street fairs at the La Quinta Village Shopping Center at the corner of Washington Street and Calle Tampico, featuring a farmers market, entertainment, and kids' activities. Fairs are held the first Friday of the winter months, starting in October, from 6 to 10pm.

"Dive-in movies" are a fun way to beat the heat at La Quinta Resort during the summer. On Saturday and Sunday nights, everybody grabs a raft and heads to the pool for a big-screen family movie with lots of popcorn.

RESTAURANTS

ADOBE GRILL ★★

Located upstairs above the hotel's famed fountain, Adobe Grill's dining patio seems almost to press against the velvet night sky. But seating accommodations aside, the menu here has long been a wonderful alternative to the steak-steak-

steak mantra of other desert chefs. Adobe Grill has an elegant, inventive, and also quite traditional touch with Mexican cuisine. Sure, you can order a combination plate (wonderful tamales, enchiladas, tacos, and the like), but it's the mysterious mole sauce where the Aztecan authenticity really shines. Seafood is a highlight, especially the halibut in a maple pecan crust with orange butter sauce. What's Mexican about it? It arrives with fideo, a Mexican pasta like angel hair or vermicelli where the thin strands are deep fried for about a minute before being doused with chicken stock, tomatoes, and herbs, then simmered until tender. *Caldo de marisco*, their bouillabaisse with a Southwest flavor, and *ceviche de mariscos marinera* also showcase Mexico's love of seafood. Don't miss the margaritas here; the largest comes in a huge handblown glass filled with 1800 tequila, orange liqueur, and fresh lime and lemon juice. *49-499 Eisenhower Dr (La Quinta Resort & Club), La Quinta; 760/564-5725; $$; AE, DIS, MC, V; no checks; lunch, dinner every day; full bar; reservations recommended; www.laquintaresort.com; from Hwy 111, take Washington St south and turn right on Eisenhower Dr.* &

LA QUINTA GRILL ★★

Arriving at La Quinta Grill will test your faith—but only from the outside. The parking lot is sand, and the building has all the architectural profile of a Texas roadhouse. But beyond the front door, you enter a big-city environment, newly remodeled and expanded. After closing for about four months in summer 2000, the bar area has been redone, and one of the dining rooms nearly doubled in size. Elegant surroundings, including crisp white tablecloths and gilt-framed paintings, belie the simple exterior. So popular in winter you may wait two hours unless you have a reservation, La Quinta Grill (once known as Cunard's) draws a clientele hungry for its wonderful chicken marsala or its popular scampi in a parsley-butter and white wine–lemon sauce. Pasta dishes, like the grilled Italian sausage tossed with generous chunks of fresh tomato, fresh basil, white wine, and shaved Parmesan, are redolent of garlic and big enough for two. Service is friendly and efficient. La Quinta Grill offers big portions and a nice atmosphere for prices about 25 percent less than if they were located "up canyon" (closer to Palm Springs). *78-045 Calle Cadiz, La Quinta; 760/564-4443; $$; AE, DC, DIS, MC, V; no checks; dinner every day; full bar; reservations recommended; from Hwy 111 go south on Washington St to 52nd Ave, right to Avenidas Bermudas, right to Calle Cadiz.* &

LODGINGS

LA QUINTA RESORT & CLUB ★★★

 The valley's second-oldest resort (it dates back to 1926) is the very definition of the classic Palm Springs–area experience. Set against a towering mountain backdrop, it boasts rambling oasis-like grounds and subdued elegance, with a Hollywood Golden Era feel of the 1920s and 1930s (Mary Pickford was a frequent guest). To this day, no other resort in the desert approaches its grand sense of place and its understated charm. Originally a cluster of 56 tile-roofed guest casitas widely spaced on lawns, the resort has grown into a large town-size complex of golf courses, tennis club, new rooms, bungalows, ballrooms, and spa—yet without losing intimacy. From the moment you drive down the long entry road between towering columnar cypresses, you feel as though you're entering a Spanish village. The casitas are almost severe in their white-walled simplicity, with thick walls, small windows, and simple furnishings, but color abounds outside, where billows of bougainvillea spill over the rooftops. Almost all have a porch for sitting in the deep shade and listening to the mariachi music float over from an evening meal at Adobe Grill. Three fine restaurants make it possible never to leave the grounds: Montañas (elegant Mediterranean), Morgans (cafe), and Adobe Grill (regional Mexican cuisine with muchas margaritas). Named one of *Tennis* magazine's Top 10 U.S. Tennis Resorts, La Quinta offers one of the most beautiful settings in the country, along with 23 courts. Add plenty of programs for the kids (Camp La Quinta), golf and tennis, and a new 23,000-square-foot spa that includes a large fitness center—with yoga and other activities and spa treatments ranging from the golfer's massage to open-air showers, warm-stone therapy, and an outdoor aromatherapy tub—and you've got a gracefully aging Eden that continues to attract entire families generation after generation. *49-499 Eisenhower Dr, La Quinta; 760/564-4111 or 800/598-3828; $$$; AE, DC, DIS, MC, V; checks OK; resinquiry@kslmail.com; www. laquintaresort.com; from Hwy 111, take Washington St south and turn right on Eisenhower Dr.* &

INDIO

The city of Indio has a rich history that goes back to the late 1800s, when the Southern Pacific Railroad designated the area, originally called Indian Wells, as a major distribution point between Yuma and Los Angeles.

More of a blue-collar community than its resort brethren just up-valley, the city supports a thriving date palm industry that goes back to the early 1900s. As the story goes, the president of the railroad, C. P. Huntington, carried back some date shoots from a vacation to Algeria during the 1880s. Sensing a great opportunity, the U.S. Department of Agriculture got into the act; date palms were planted throughout the area, and by 1914 growers had formed the Coachella Valley Date Growers Association.

The largest community in the Coachella Valley with approximately 45,000 year-round residents, Indio is still known for acres of date farms and shops selling the ever-popular date shake. But Indio has also earned a place on the map as the host of the crowd-pleasing Skins Game golf tournament, where four pros compete for big money on each hole, and as the home to the Fantasy Springs Casino. It also offers two big attractions for horse lovers: a major annual equestrian event, and two polo clubs.

For more information, contact the Indio Chamber of Commerce (82-503 Hwy 111; 760/347-0676 or 800/44-INDIO; www.indiochamber.org).

ACTIVITIES

Indio Desert Circuit Horse Show. The edge-of-your-seat spectator sport of show jumping comes to Indio for six weeks every January, attracting first-class horses and riders from throughout the nation. Along with Grand Prix show-jumping—a timed event featuring enormous fences, tightly arranged courses,

stunningly gorgeous horseflesh, and some serious prize money—
the circuit features other English riding competitions in 10 different rings. Indio attracts plenty of Olympic-caliber talent,
including trainers and riders who flock to these prestigious show
grounds for a shot at over $1 million in prizes, and horses whose
prices can reach six figures. Even if the closest you've ever come to
the equine world is a day at the track or a game of horseshoes, the
high-flying Grand Prix events, held on Fridays and Sundays, are
well worth your time. Admission is free Wednesday through Friday; $5 Saturday and Sunday; free for kids 12 and under. (81-500
Avenue 52, at Monroe St and Avenue 52; 760/775-7731;
www.hitsshows.com.)

 Indian casino. The Fantasy Springs Casino, run by the
Cabazon band of Mission Indians, is open 24/7 for live
blackjack and poker tables, off-track betting, and bingo, as well as
video gaming machines. It also hosts outdoor concerts (country
western, salsa, rock 'n' roll, you name it) and boxing matches.
There's a bowling alley, too: 24 lanes with a full bar, snacks, and
extended hours (9am–2am daily). (84-245 Indio Springs Dr;
760/342-5000; www.cabazonindians.com; from I-10 take Golf
Center Pkwy north to Indio Springs Dr and go east.)

Polo grounds. Two adjacent clubs have partnered to
make Indio one of the hotbeds of polo in the U.S. At the
Eldorado Polo Club, which has more than a dozen playing fields,
visitors can watch amateur and professional polo players and
their glistening "ponies" speed across the fields in pursuit of
glory, prizes, and a small, hard bamboo ball. The club's season
runs from November through April and attracts an international
set of players—Princes Philip and Charles of England have both
played here. Spectators are welcome, and admission starts at
approximately $6. Call ahead for information about tickets, tour-
nament dates, and polo lessons. (50-950 Madison St, near Madison St and Avenue 50; 760/342-2223.)

Nearby is the Empire Polo Club, a gorgeous private club where
players from around the world come to play on three sprawling,
well-tended polo fields. Unbeknownst to most valley visitors, the
club is home to one of the more stunning event venues in the
entire country, Medjool Lake. Like a secret garden for the rich,
this expansive walled retreat has winding paths, an enormous

A standard polo field is 300 yards by 160 yards (that's roughly six football fields), with the goalposts set 8 yards apart.

Polo is played in chukkers, not halves or innings. A chukker is 7 min-utes long, and there are typically six chukkers in a game.

pond, sculptures, patios, and beautiful gardens. It overlooks one of the polo fields, where exhibition matches are often held for corporate parties. It's also the home of golf-cart polo, in which mallet-bearing guests take a whack at the sport from carts driven by real polo players.

A number of America's biggest corporations have held parties on these grounds, which also host concerts and musical festivals. Pearl Jam played here in 1993, while the two-day Coachella Fest, featuring alternative rock and attended by 55,000 fans, was held here in October 1999. (81-800 Avenue 51; 760/342-2762; empire polo@aol.com; from I-10 take the Monroe St exit and go south about 3.8 miles; pass Avenue 50 and at the sign Empire Polo Club turn right on a dirt road, which is Avenue 51.)

 Indio International Tamale Festival. Tamales, prepared with cornmeal and fillings ranging from shredded meat to dried fruit, are a traditional holiday food in Mexico, where both savory and sweet tamales are prepared around Christmastime. This two-day festival, which began in 1992, salutes the holiday season with tamale-cooking contests, about 70 tamale vendors—each, it seems, with a different recipe—and a parade. In 1999, the event drew an estimated crowd of more than 100,000. Always held the first week in December, the festival itself is free—though you'll need to buy the tamales. To get to the festival, take Interstate 10 to the Monroe Street exit and then south to Highway 111. Turn east at Highway 111 to Oasis Street (about 3 blocks) and turn north on Oasis. A few blocks down on the right side watch for the signs, banners, and the festival itself (760/342-6532; www.tamalefestival.org).

Dates are fat-free snacks that have more potassium (by weight) than bananas. You can store them for a month in the refrigerator, up to a year in the freezer.

National Date Festival. Indio's most famous event celebrates the date groves that were planted here in the early 1900s and now produce the majority of the nation's dates. Each February, the festival comes to the Riverside County Fairgrounds (46-350 Arabia St; 760/863-8247) for 10 days of food and fun. Concerts and classic carnival rides are joined by exhibit halls crammed with fruits, vegetables, art exhibits, industrial arts, fossilized blue-ribbon pies—you know, all the classic fair accoutrements.

DATE PALMS

It's estimated that 95 percent of all dates grown in the United States come from Indio and the surrounding Coachella Valley. Production is about 40 million pounds per year. Although countless varieties of dates are grown in Indio, the most popular are the Deglet Noor ("date of light"), Barhi, Zahidi, and Medjool. The harvest season begins in mid-August and continues into December, and is celebrated each February with Indio's National Date Festival. Although date palms are hardy enough to survive in the desert, they require enormous amounts of water and attention to thrive. The costs associated with irrigating, pollinating, and harvesting the dates are one reason they've been prized throughout history and continue to demand top prices today. Guess there's no such thing as a cheap date.

Make your own date shake with a recipe provided by Hadley Fruit Orchards: In a blender, combine ¼ cup of chopped pitted dates with ¼ cup of milk. Blend until creamy. Add another ¾ cup of milk and 3 cups of vanilla ice cream or ice milk. Blend to desired thickness. Makes 3 servings.

Indio Open-Air Market. Shoppers, browsers, and bargainers converge twice a week, year-round, for this outdoor bazaar. Held from 4 to 10pm on Wednesdays and Saturdays, the market is devoted to new and used stuff of all kinds. In addition to vendors selling merchandise, the event includes a number of food booths. (46-350 Arabia St, at the Riverside County and National Date Festival Grounds; 800/222-7467.)

DESERT HOT SPRINGS AND INDIAN WELLS

DESERT HOT SPRINGS

No mystery surrounds the naming of this town, which lies north of Palm Springs off Highway 10. It's home to about 40 hot-springs spas, which devotees swear have medicinal properties. Most commonly touted as a remedy for arthritis and rheumatism, the steaming mineral water bubbles up at an average of 140 to 150°F, perfect for filling the various pools, soaking tubs, and private bathtubs offered at the local motels and resorts. Most of these offer day rates for those who just want to drop in for a few hours, as well as treatments such as massage, facials, body wraps, and aromatherapy. Interestingly enough, the Desert Hot Springs cold water provides its own magic: Delectably pure, it's won a number of drinking water competitions.

Most people know Desert Hot Springs only as home to Two Bunch Palms, a luxurious retreat that played a prominent part in the Robert Altman film *The Player* (Tim Robbins and Greta Scacchi fled L.A. to lounge in one of the resort's mud baths). Indeed, Two Bunch Palms, with its celebrity guest list and ban on loud conversations and annoying cell phones, is a dream destination for anyone with the wherewithal to afford a stay there. But the town is also home to about 15,000 people, and while there isn't much to do here, that's just the point. This desert hamlet nestled at the foot of the Little San Bernardino Mountains is a place to slow down, take the waters, and, if you're feeling ambitious, read a good book.

LODGINGS

DESERT HOT SPRINGS RESORT AND SPA ☆

Although this resort resembles your basic motor hotel, with plain two-story buildings wrapped around a courtyard, it's quite popular and makes a decent place to stay, especially if you have children. Service is friendly and accommodating, and the patio area and pools, sheltered by palm trees, look immaculate. Many of the guest rooms overlook the pool, with sliding glass doors that open onto small balconies or patios. For more privacy, choose the upstairs accommodations; if you have kids who will be running in and out, go for the pool-facing ground floor. The simply decorated rooms

Not sure how to "take the waters" in Desert Hot Springs? Some experts recommend the "three dip method." Sit in a hot-water spa for 5 to 10 minutes before exiting to cool off for a few minutes. Enter the hot spa again for 5 minutes, then take a dip in the cooler swimming pool. Finally, hit the spa again for 5 minutes before drying off and lying down to rest. Aaaah.

are nothing fancy, but have comfortable king- or queen-size beds, minifridges, and fair-sized baths. Soaking and sunning options here are many, with an Olympic-size pool and several smaller spas with mineral waters ranging from warm to hot. Water aerobics classes are offered (call ahead for a schedule), there's a snack bar right by the pool, and one wing of the resort is devoted to facials, massage, and other body work. Nonguests may buy day-use pool permits, including a locker and towel, for about $5. *10-805 Palm Dr, Desert Hot Springs; 760/329-6000 or 800/808-7727; $; AE, DC, DIS, MC, V; no checks; from I-10, go north on Palm Dr past Pierson and 8th Sts, hotel is on the left (before Miracle Springs).*

MIRACLE SPRINGS RESORT AND SPA ★★

 Just up the street from the Desert Hot Springs Resort and Spa, this sister property has a grander, newer appearance, though it's not what we'd call a luxury hotel. Still, it's quite attractive, with a pretty lobby area, sizeable restaurant and lounge (a big positive, since Desert Hot Springs isn't long on dining options), and an atrium room that can be reserved for meetings and special events. Guest rooms are furnished in restful, neutral tones with a choice of king or two double beds in the standard accommodations. Some larger suites have two TVs and a sitting area with sofa, and a few include a minifridge. Accommodations overlooking the pool, with their own small balconies or patios, cost a bit more than the mountain-facing rooms but are worth it for the oasis-like scene of pools and palm trees. In addition to the main swimming pool, the hotel boasts several hot mineral soaking pools (we saw one blissed-out couple with their chaise lounges resting *in* the shallow waters) and offers spa services. A tip about the latter: Customers can save a few dollars by ordering spa package deals that combine several services; check with the hotel or its Web site for prices and specifics. *10-625 Palm Dr, Desert Hot Springs; 800/400-4414; $; AE, DC, DIS, MC, V; checks OK; hotel@miraclesprings.com; www.miraclesprings.com; from I-10, go north on Palm Dr past Pierson and 8th Sts, hotel is on the left.* ♿

TWO BUNCH PALMS ⋆⋆⋆

Water is precious enough in the desert, but when it rises, steaming and full of minerals from deep in the earth into an oasis of palm trees, you have the makings of a classic hot-springs spa. Accommodations are 45 casitas scattered throughout the lawns, linked by pathways and furnished with antiques and rattan; only guests have access to the almost 60 acres of landscaped grounds. The property is exceedingly quiet and private. You can choose either a simple resort stay or an immersion in the spa's full program of massage treatments, sauna, mud baths, and body wrap treatments. Serenity is the watchword here; in the mineral hot springs, even conversations among guests are kept to a whisper. And what springs! Landscaped for a grotto effect, the pools are rock-lined, rambling organic forms nestled amidst the palm trunks for an absolutely magical experience. Resort or spa packages can include meals, treatments, and even "romance" treatments, which feature side-by-side massages, Roman tub baths by candlelight, and private mud- and sun-baskings on a sundeck. Nude sunbathing is encouraged in special private "sun bins." When guests want a bit more activity, they can play tennis (two courts), work out in the exercise pool, walk trails around the property, or ride a bicycle. Lodgings range from guest rooms equipped with minifridges and cable TV (some, with private patio) to spacious suites and villas with separate dining areas, minikitchens, and whirlpool spas. Decor and furnishings tend toward a relaxed, Southwest style that encourages lounging about. The Casino Dining Room features "Living Essence Cuisine," and although the name is somewhat egregious, the low-fat, "strictly fresh" fare is excellent. The restaurant has a full bar and a good selection of wines. Meals are included in rate packages, and a two-night minimum is required. Note: Check the rates during July and August, when they often drop by 50 percent for first-time visitors. *67-425 Two Bunch Palms Trail, Desert Hot Springs; 760/329-8791; $$$–$$$$; AE, MC, V; no checks; www.twobunchpalms.com; left off Hwy 10's Desert Hot Springs exit 5 miles north to Two Bunch Palms Trail.* ⅃

Before you climb into a hot-water spa, check the temperature. The mineral waters bubble up from underground at anywhere between 90 and 150°F.

NASTY ANTS

Ah, the familiar hazards of the desert: Rattlers. Scorpions. Tarantulas. Ants.

Ants?

Indeed—the biting, stinging, markedly aggressive variety known as the red imported fire ant. Colonies of this species, which originated in South America, have been found in various parts of Riverside County, including Palm Desert, Rancho Mirage, Palm Springs, and Indio. While they're certainly not as big a problem as they are in the southern United States, they're nasty enough to rate an eradication campaign and several quarantined areas in California.

Although physically they resemble your regular garden variety ant, fire ants are quick to attack by the hundreds—or thousands—if disturbed. According to Larry Cooper at the California Department of Food and Agriculture, a number of people living in the Coachella Valley area have been stung, some severely.

"The reason these things are of concern is that if they perceive a threat to their mound, if you get too close or step on it, they're very fast and will swarm right up your leg," Cooper explained. "While they're biting you, they rotate and sting you repeatedly in circles." The ant stings result in painful white blisters that can easily become infected. Worse, about 1 percent of the population suffers serious allergic reactions to the venom. Finally, the ants can be especially dangerous to babies and toddlers, small pets, and newborn livestock that can't escape them.

Cooper says the ants are attracted by water and often build their distinctive mounds along the edges of lawns, on golf courses, along curbs, or near swimming pools. (They also tend to swarm in electrical connections, in laundry rooms, and occasionally in washing machines.) The mounds start out as small piles of very fine sand or sifted dirt and can grow up to a foot high.

Fortunately, it's not difficult to avoid fire ants, and they're certainly not out there stalking anyone. Many desert residents have never even seen a fire ant. Anyone who does get stung should immediately wash or brush the ants off, treat the affected area with antiseptic, and report the location of the mound to the Fire Ant Hotline (800/491-1899).

INDIAN WELLS

Welcome to one of the valley's upper-crust neighborhoods, indeed, to one of the richest cities in the state of California. This quiet refuge for the super-rich has a median household income of about $110,000, and it's estimated that 75 percent of Indian Wells's residents dwell behind guarded gates. Homeowners here include Bill Gates, John Elway, and Lee Iacocca. Indian Wells is also the site of the uber-exclusive Vintage Club, a golf resort where, according to a recent article in *Forbes* magazine, the initiation fee alone is $300K.

However, no one's going to check your net worth if you're just coming to visit. The area is home to several deluxe hotels where accommodations can be downright cheap during the summer. And no matter what time of year it is, the last time we checked, walking, window-shopping, and looking around were free.

ACTIVITIES

Tennis masters. The Tennis Master Series Indian Wells Tournament, held in the spiffy new Indian Wells Tennis Gardens, attracts top-ranked players from around the world every March. Both one-day and series tickets are available to the public. For details about the tournament, as well as information about membership in the Indian Wells Tennis Gardens club, see the "Tennis, Anyone?" sidebar on page 42.

RESTAURANTS

LE ST. GERMAIN ★★

This relative of the vaunted Le Vallauris in Palm Springs offers a rather similar menu of updated French cuisine in a relaxed, low-key setting. A minimalist mural of Paris's Ile de la Cité dominates one wall in the main dining room, a brightly lit space with a view of everyone who comes and goes. Given the lack of cozy nooks and crannies, romantics may prefer to sit in the slightly more protected patio surrounded by greenery, or have a tête-à-tête at the bar. The menu encompasses a number of French classics, such as sautéed foie gras, steamed mussels, and dessert souffles, as well as California menu standards like swordfish, ahi, pastas, and filet mignon. Best bets are the seared duck breast seasoned with caramelized shallots (although the accompanying foie gras was scant indeed), crab cakes, and the lush porcini-stuffed ravioli flavored with truffle oil. Service ranges from skilled to a bit haphazard (we really shouldn't have to tell our server that the entrees he's carrying belong two tables over). The wine list, while quite expensive, is extensive enough to have garnered an award of excellence from *Wine Spectator* magazine. Expect to pay at least $40 for a good-to-very-good chard or cabernet. *74-985 Hwy 111, Indian Wells; 760/773-6511 or 888/304-7999; $$; AE, DIS, MC, V; no checks, lunch, dinner every day; full bar; reservations recommended; Stgermain@lestgermain.com; www.lestgermain. com; near Cook St.*

LODGINGS

HYATT GRAND CHAMPIONS ★★★

One look at the spacious, split-level standard suites at this grandiose hotel, and you'll be tempted to check in immediately. A glimpse of the deluxe, top-floor penthouse suites or the captivating private villas (the latter complete with personal butler), and you'll be tempted to move in permanently. Comfort is the name of the game: Even the standard suites include generous square footage, sofas, minibars, work desks, plush robes, and ironing boards, along with bathrooms larger than some studio apartments. Move up to the top-floor penthouse rooms, and you'll also get a fireplace, spacious balcony, separate bedroom, and a couple of bathrooms. The top-priced villas set in walled "compounds" of four are like separate worlds unto themselves, with covered parking, marble entryways, enormous sitting rooms and bedrooms, a fireplace, and private garden patios, each with a Jacuzzi. The rest of the hotel is equally impressive, from the thoughtfully landscaped pool areas, abloom with native plants and home to five swimming pools, to the well-groomed grounds and tennis courts. Camp Hyatt offers activities for kids, while the Spa Hyatt promises to pamper adults from head to toe (especially welcome after a few sessions at the well-equipped fitness center). Oh, and don't forget the two 18-hole championship golf courses. The lobby and other public areas can feel a bit crowded and impersonal, but once you're in your own room or sheltered in a cabana by the pool, it's heaven. *44-600 Indian Wells Ln, Indian Wells; 760/341-1000 or 800/554-9288; $$$; AE, DC, DIS, MC, V; no checks; www.grand champions.hyatt.com; off Hwy 111.* &

INDIAN WELLS RESORT HOTEL   ★★

Although it's not as grand as its sprawling resort neighbors across the street, this older hotel is comfortable enough, and offers several nice touches. Stays here include a free continental breakfast with fresh fruit, cereals, and baked goods, as well as a complimentary happy hour each night that includes beer, wine, or other adult beverages along with snacks. The pool is immaculate, with a separate raised whirlpool, and while the outdoor tennis courts have seen better days, they're playable and free to guests. The low, low rates here during the summer (as little as $59 for a decent room with two queen beds) make it a favorite of golfers, who can walk to the three nearby courses. Be sure to request a room overlooking the pool and golf course, rather than one facing the parking lot and Highway 111. Rooms are simply furnished, with mass-produced art and basic furniture; no bathrobes or extensive collection of travel-sized amenities here. Still, the service is pleasant and friendly, and the pace more relaxed than at some of the megahotels. In addition to the standard rooms, the hotel also offers a number of larger suites, including the Big Daddy of 'em all: the 4,500-square-foot presidential suite. *76-661 Hwy 111, Indian Wells; 760/345-6466 or 800/248-3220; $$$; AE, DC, DIS, MC, V; checks OK; info@indianwellsresort.com; www.indian wellsresort.com; off Hwy 111.* &

MIRAMONTE RESORT   ★★★

A taste of *bella* Tuscany came to Indian Wells in 1998, when the old Erawan Garden hotel was renovated (to the tune of $25 million) and renamed the Miramonte Resort. From the cobblestone driveway and tastefully grand lobby to the pristine lawns and gardens, the place radiates Old World charm. Although the resort offers about 225 rooms in 14 tile-roofed "villas," it manages to project an intimate, exclusive atmosphere. The grounds are intersected by winding paths bordered with flowers, with the occasional bench seat or neatly trimmed lawn practically insisting you sit down and smell the roses for a while. The main swimming pool is anchored at one end by a cascade of bougainvillea, and surrounded by chaise lounges and a handful of chic white cabanas. The latter are fitted with minirefrigerators, and guests can also request telephone service to their cabanas. But who wants to be connected to the outside world when there are tanned bodies to observe, bird songs to enjoy, and tropical drinks to sip? As for the rooms, they're as smashing as the rest of the property. Even the basic rooms are spacious and carefully appointed, with big marble bathrooms, wrought iron king- or queen-size beds, plenty of lamps, individual balconies or patios, and soothing terra-cotta color schemes. Lots of businesspeople stay here during conventions, and so do some families with children and dogs (pets are allowed). But at its heart, the Miramonte looks like it was really designed for couples and romance, to which we say *bravo!* The hotel offers 24-hour room service, as well as the Ristorante Brissago, home to rotisserie-grilled meats, antipasti of all kinds, pastas, salads, fresh fish, and, of course, wines from Italy. *45-000 Indian Wells Ln, Indian Wells; 760/341-2200 or 800/237-2926; $, AE, DC, DIS, MC, V; checks OK; info@miramonteresort.com; www.miramonteresort.com; just off Hwy 111.* &

RENAISSANCE ESMERALDA RESORT ★★★

 Taking its architectural cue from the surrounding peaks, Renaissance Esmeralda is a series of mountainous, but dramatically modern and stylish buildings organized around a central courtyard shaded by stately Canary Island palms. The courtyard's centerpiece is an immense pool complete with a sandy beach that actually slopes into the water. The 560 rooms and suites amidst seven-story buildings are some of the largest in the valley. All have private balconies and are decorated in schemes of mauve that echo

the mountains' hues at sunset. Deluxe rooms include corner arrangements with windows on two walls, but one of
the pair is behind a disconcerting grid that's part of the
exterior ornamentation. Ask for a room with a view of the
mountains to the west, or at the very least to the north or
south; east-side rooms have a much less interesting vista.
Esmeralda's soaring atrium lobby is too huge to be friendly,
and the decor is unabashedly ritzy. But with two 18-hole
championship golf courses designed by Ted Robinson, Sr.,
extensive health club and spa services, four tennis courts,
and in-room coffee and newspaper every morning, no
one's complaining. The Sirocco restaurant, featuring
Mediterranean cuisine, is one of the prettiest spaces for
dining in the desert. Overall, service at Esmeralda is polished and worldly, as befits a hotel that hosts major corporate functions. On the other hand, the place can feel too
businesslike for the vacationing family—despite its sandy
beach. *44-400 Indian Wells Ln, Indian Wells; 760/773-4444
or 800/552-4386; $$$$; AE, DC, DIS, JCB, MC, V; no checks;
www.renaissancehotels.com; located off Hwy 111.* &

SALTON SEA

SALTON SEA

Thirty-five miles long and 15 miles wide, the Salton Sea lies about 30 miles southeast of Indio. This salty body of water is surrounded by the Santa Rosa Mountains to the west, the Superstition Mountains to the southwest, Imperial Valley and Mexicali to the south, and the Chocolate Mountains to the east. Just southeast of the Salton Sea is the small community of Calipatria; from there, Brawley and El Centro lie to the south.

The Salton Sea is a bird-watcher's fantasy sprung to life, since it's located between two major migratory flyways and is the nesting ground to countless birds. It's also a recreational fishing area, and a draw for boaters, campers, and hikers.

The Sea is nearly 227 feet below sea level, only 5 feet higher than the lowest point in Death Valley. It was once the bottom of a prehistoric sea, back when the Gulf of California extended north into what are now the Imperial and Coachella Valleys. A giant upthrust in the area resulted in the formation of the nearby mountains. Eventually, silt deposited by the Colorado River formed a delta that closed off the northern arm of the basin from the gulf, but every so often, the river overflowed and filled the valley between the mountain ranges.

From 1828 to 1904, the Colorado River flooded the Salton Basin no fewer than eight times. It was dry when the Imperial Canal was completed in 1901. The canal diverted water for irrigation from the Colorado River just up from the Mexican border. But heavy winter rains in 1905 caused massive flooding that eventually broke the canal. For 15 months, the entire flow of the Colorado River poured through Mexicali and Imperial Valley and into the Salton Sink. Farms and homes were imperiled, but later saved when the river break was fixed in the spring of 1907. What was left was a new lake, renamed the Salton Sea.

Today, the Sea covers 376 square miles, almost twice the size of Lake Tahoe. It reaches a depth of about 50 feet, but is no more than 10 feet deep in many areas. Currently, it's almost 30 percent saltier than ocean water.

Over the last few decades, the Sea has struggled to survive. A lack of oxygen, overabundance of algae, and increasing salinity has caused massive fish kills here, especially of tilapia, a fish that resembles a bluegill. The massive die-offs have resulted in spreads of botulism that have led to catastrophic bird kills. All that has given the Sea a terrible reputation, not to mention a foul smell that drove recreationalists away in the 1970s and 1980s.

A Salton Sea Task Force was formed in 1986, joining together all the various agencies charged with the Sea's management and stewardship. Their goals are simple: Find workable solutions to stabilize the elevation and salinity of the Sea.

Despite its problems, the Sea is a vital ecological resource. And, it remains a viable recreation area, attracting as many as 275,000 visitors each year.

The Salton Sea State Recreation Area has 1,400 campsites in five campgrounds with hundreds of picnic sites, trails, playgrounds, boat ramps, and a visitor center. It's a favorite for boaters, offering good fishing (if the wind isn't blowing or it isn't too hot), waterskiing, sailboarding, jet skiing, hiking, and, of course, birding. It's also home to an estimated 200 million fish; the most common species are orangemouth corvina, sargo, tilapia, and croaker.

The main routes to the Sea are Interstate 10 and Interstate 8. Highways 111 and 86 (east of Indio) go south to the Sea, and Highway 111 runs along the entire east shoreline. Highway 86 runs down the west shoreline. For more information about this area, contact Salton Sea State Recreation Area (760/393-3052).

ACTIVITIES

Bird-watching. The combination of open water, salt marshes, freshwater ponds, and desert scrub near and around the Salton Sea makes it a magnet for birds. More than 380 species of the 900 known to exist in North America have been spotted here. Some of the rarer sightings include flamingo, brown booby, and frigatebird. Resident birds include greater roadrunners, Gambel's quail, and the endangered Yuma clapper rail. And every year, multitudes of feathered visitors stop at the Sea as they travel the Pacific Flyway. Egrets, plovers, brown pelicans, and American white pelicans are just a few of the common species seen in fall. You'll also find thousands of Canada geese, snow geese, and Ross's geese, as well as northern pintails and other ducks such as green-winged teal, cinnamon teal, and mallards. Shorebirds can be seen year-round, especially in the fall and spring. Fall and early winter are the best times to see migrating varieties.

 Annual bird fest. Each February, the region sponsors the annual Salton Sea International Bird Festival. This four-day event draws enthusiasts from throughout the country for seminars and presentations by nationally known birders, scientists, and biologists, as well as local wildlife and water experts. A trade show, tours, and field trips, some of them geared toward children, round out the schedule. For information, contact the El Centro Chamber of Commerce and Visitors Bureau (760/352-3681; generalinfo@elcentrochamber.com; www.el centrochamber.com).

 Fishing. The prize fish of the Salton Sea is the orange-mouth corvina, which can be as big as 37 pounds, though most are in the 2- to 10-pound range. Boat fishermen generally catch bigger fish in the winter in deep water, but shore anglers often hook into quality catches, especially those who wade out for some "armpit fishing," the practice of wading up to one's armpits and fishing from out there. Corvina seek shallow water in the spring and early summer, but then go deep for cooler water as the desert temperatures rise.

Tilapia are native to the Middle East and Africa and are prolific breeders. They average between one-half pound to 3 pounds in size and can be caught on night crawlers or red-worms. Experts advise attaching a kernel of corn on the hook with the worm to attract the fish. The sargo ranges from one-half pound to 2 pounds and hangs out around submerged structures such as buildings, trees, or jetties. Try the jetty at the Salton Sea State Recreation Area for sargo.

 Hiking. Keep in mind that temperatures in the area can be brutally high during the summer, well over 100°F. Water, sunscreen, hat. It's the desert hiker's mantra.

Hikes around the Sonny Bono Salton Sea National Wildlife Refuge will almost always turn up some great views of wildlife. One hike, the ***Rock Creek Trail*** (easy, 3-mile round-trip), on the east shore of the Sea, is a fine way to take advantage of the Sea's great bird-watching. It leads from the observation platform behind the visitor center to a path along the levee and stops atop

Note to anglers: The vibrio bacteria, common to saltwater environments, is sometimes present in fish from the Salton Sea. Although it can cause illness in humans, it isn't considered a serious health threat if the fish are not allowed to spoil and are cooked promptly. Keep fish on ice to keep them from spoiling, and never eat raw fish from the Sea.

a hill above the Sea. From Indio, go south on Highway 111 for about 50 miles to Sinclair Road, 4 miles south of Niland. Go right on Sinclair Road for 6 miles to the Refuge Visitor Center, located at Sinclair Road and Gentry Road.

The **Michael Hardenberger Trail** (easy, 0.5-mile loop) is at Unit 1 of the Sonny Bono Salton Sea National Wildlife Refuge. There's an observation platform that overlooks the Sea, and a photography blind in the middle of a pond on this trail off Vendel Road. Take Highway 78/86 east to Vendel Road, and go 1 mile to the Unit 1 area.

Camping. Headquarters Camp has 40 sites for tents and RVs (15 with full hookups; maximum RV length 32 feet). Facilities include picnic tables, barbecue grills, drinking water, flush toilets, showers, dump station, and a boat launch. There's also a small playground for the kids, a visitor center and a 1-mile-long, self-guided nature trail that hugs the shoreline from Headquarters Camp to Mecca Beach Campground. This popular campground fills up fast, so be sure to make reservations. Stay limit is 30 days, and it's open all year. Good swimming, fishing, boating, hiking, and waterskiing. From Indio, head south on

WILDLIFE REFUGE

The Sonny Bono Salton Sea National Wildlife Refuge (760/348-5278) was officially named after the late congressman in 1998 in honor of his efforts to help preserve the lake. The area was created by presidential proclamation back in the '30s. It is composed of more than 36,500 acres at the southern end of the Salton Sea, although most of the refuge has been inundated by the Sea's rising waters. The present refuge is a narrow corridor of land that borders the Sea, with farmed crops and native marsh to provide habitat for wintering waterfowl. Bird-watchers who come here will be richly rewarded. The refuge is northwest of Calipatria (which lies between the south end of the Salton Sea and Brawley), and is open from dawn till dusk. From Calipatria head north 5 miles on Highway 111, then go left (west) on Sinclair Road 6 miles to refuge headquarters. It also can be reached from Highway 86/78 by taking Forrester Road (Gentry Road) north to Sinclair and the refuge entrance.

Highway 111 to the town of Mecca; from Mecca, go 10 miles southeast on Highway 111 to the campground; 800/444-7275.

Mecca Beach Campground has 110 sites for tents and RVs (no hookups; maximum RV length 30 feet). Facilities include picnic tables, fire rings, drinking water, flush toilets, and showers. Trees provide some respite from the sun. Stay limit is 30 days; open year-round; fee required. From Mecca, go 11.5 miles southeast on Highway 111 to the campground entrance on the northeastern side of the lake; 800/444-7275.

Corvina Beach Campground offers primitive camping for tents and RVs (no hookups; maximum RV length 32 feet). Amenities include only the bare essentials: drinking water, chemical toilets, and a boat ramp. Open all year, with a stay limit of 30 days; fee required. From Mecca, go 14 miles southeast on Highway 111 to the campground entrance on the Salton Sea side of the highway; 800/444-7275.

Salt Creek Campground is known for offering excellent birding at the mouth of Salt Creek. Fishing is also said to be quite good here. Sites for tents and RVs (no hookups; no maximum RV length). Drinking water and chemical toilets here. Open all year, with a stay limit of 30 days; fee required. From Mecca, go 17 miles southeast on Highway 111; 800/444-7275.

Bombay Beach Campground is the southernmost site in the recreation area. It has 200 sites for tents and RVs (no hookups; no maximum RV length). It does have drinking water and chemical toilets. Open all year, with a stay limit of 30 days; fee required. From Mecca, go 27 miles southeast on Highway 111; 800/444-7275.

Red Hill Marina County Park has 400 sites for tents and RVs, a few with electrical hookups (no maximum RV length). This area has been upgraded and is in very good condition. Amenities include picnic tables, barbecue grills, drinking water, flush toilets, showers, boat ramp, and loading dock. A fine setting along the southeastern shore of the Salton Sea makes this a favorite for boaters and campers. And, it's only 3.6 miles from the Salton Sea National Wildlife Refuge. Open all year, with a stay limit of 14 days; fee required. From the intersection of Noffsinger Road and Highway 111 in Niland, take Highway 111 south for 5 miles. Go right onto Sinclair Road and drive 4.5 miles to Garst Road. Turn

Check with the state park rangers at the Sea to find out about their lecture series, campfire programs, bird-watching expeditions, and junior ranger programs for kids.

right on Garst Road and go 1.5 miles to Red Hill Road. Turn left and follow Red Hill Road to the campground; 760/348-2310.

Boating. Although many boaters take to the Salton Sea simply to catch a few fish, some serious speeding goes on here as well. The Sea is known as the fastest boat-racing lake in the nation because its high salt content causes vessels to be more buoyant. Brisk winds also make the lake a favored spot for sailboarders in search of a good rush. Be aware, however, that since the Sea is fairly shallow, sudden strong winds can create swells from 3 to 6 feet high. High winds are most likely November through April, although they can occur at any time of year. If winds begin to rise, rangers advise that all boaters return to shore.

Boat ramps are available throughout the Salton Sea shoreline. The Desert Shores Marina (west shore) is reached by taking Interstate 10 to Highway 111. Go south on Highway 111 to Highway 86 and head south to the resort at Desert Shores; 760/395-5280.

Red Hill Marina (on the east shore) also can be reached from Interstate 10. Take the Highway 111 turnoff south through Niland to St. Clair Road. Go right for 3.5 miles to Garst Road. Turn right and go 1.5 miles to the marina; 760/348-2310.

Golf. Del Rio Country Club (102 East Del Rio Rd; 760/344-0085), northwest of Brawley, is an 18-hole championship golf course that weaves through a maze of palms and eucalyptus trees. Take Interstate 10 to Indio, then take Highway 111 south. The course is 2 miles north of Brawley.

THE HIGH
DESERT

THE HIGH DESERT

The Mojave Desert stretches for hundreds of thousands of acres to the north and east of Palm Springs. Known as the high desert, this area averages 3,000 feet in elevation—the lowest elevation at which the shaggy, spectacular Joshua Tree will grow.

In the land of the Joshua Tree, three things are certain: It will get infernally hot, it will snow, and these spiky-leafed, multi-armed trees will survive summer's griddle heat and winter's occasional snow flurries and icy winds. They've been here for hundreds of years; records claim that the trees were named by Mormons who traveled through the desert during the 1850s. (It's said that the spreading, expressive branches reminded them of the biblical figure Joshua, showing them to the Promised Land.) Researchers estimate that the oldest trees in the park may be from 500 to more than 1,000 years old.

The entire region, like the Joshua Tree, embodies characteristics of improbable hardiness and subtle surprises. Enlightened visitors willing to log some long, hard miles on interstates and backroads will discover—through the windshield, on a day hike, or especially from a towering granite edge or the rim of a slumbering desert volcano—that the high desert is a celebration of immensity, of emptiness, of quiet so intense you can hear your heart beating.

Two major east-west interstates lead to Joshua Tree. From the south, the Cottonwood Spring Visitor Center and Cottonwood entrance can be reached by taking Interstate 15 to Interstate 215 and then going east on Interstate 10. Exit 24 miles east of Indio on Cottonwood Spring Road and go 1 mile to the Cottonwood entrance. From the west, the Cottonwood entrance is 52 miles east of Palm Springs. Go north 1 mile on Cottonwood Spring Road to the southern boundary. To reach the north entrance and Oasis Visitors Center, from the west, take Interstate 10 and go 16 miles east of Banning, take Highway 62 north to Yucca Valley, Joshua Tree, and Twentynine Palms. The Oasis Visitor Center is 0.5 mile south of Highway 62 in Twentynine Palms. From the east on Interstate 10, go 45 miles west of Blythe. From the north, reach the park by taking Interstate 40 to Ludlow, exit there and go south through Amboy, 50 miles to the park's visitor center and north entrance. The park also has a west entrance; take Highway 62 into

Sudden storms can turn a bone-dry desert into a land of rushing waters that can sweep away pedestrians and cars. Stay out of all narrow canyons and washes when the weather is threatening or raining. Be alert for lightning, especially in open areas. Storms can arrive quickly and unexpectedly, and even a cloudburst can cause flooding in the desert, where the water runs off rather than sinking into the sand.

Most high-desert campers prefer to stay in Joshua Tree National Park. However, free primitive camping is available at Morongo Valley Park, 5 miles north of Big Morongo on Highway 62.

the town of Joshua Tree and turn south on Park Boulevard to reach the entrance. Note: The terms Highway 62 and Twentynine Palms Highway are often used interchangeably in this area.

MORONGO VALLEY

Named after the Morongo Indians, who once inhabited the area, this pretty little valley is just 17 miles north of Palm Springs. And at 2,500 feet elevation, it's enough to make your ears pop as you leave the desert floor. The town looks tiny, especially to visitors just passing through on the way to or from Joshua Tree or Twentynine Palms. That's simply because most residents live in houses well off the highway. As you're driving through, keep your eyes peeled for such local landmarks as Cactus Mart. This specialty nursery, on the right side of the road just past Park Avenue, has a sign that invites visitors to "Dig Your Own Cactus—39 cents." If you decide to take advantage of the low price, be sure to bring your own gloves. Cultural note: "Dig Your Own Cactus" is also the name of a popular band based in Joshua Tree.

ACTIVITIES

Big Morongo Canyon Preserve. Big Morongo Canyon is well worth a stop and a hike, especially if you're a bird-watcher. Experts consider this one of the 10 best bird-watching spots in all of California—293 species have been seen here. You may see a vermilion flycatcher or a beautiful blue grosbeak, and a flash of red might well be a summer tanager. Rare or endangered species such as the Least Bell's Vireo have also been spotted. From October to May, an experienced birder leads tours on Wednesday mornings; call the phone number below for details. The preserve also attracts bighorn sheep, bobcats, raccoons, and coyotes, along with a number of rodents and snakes. Water from the mountains seeps down to create a flourishing marsh crossed and skirted by trails, including a boardwalk that plunges through a veritable tunnel of greenery. A number of hiking trails begin at the park kiosk, ranging in length from 0.3 mile to a 12-mile round-trip. Note: No dogs allowed. Open every day 7:30am to sunset; free admission. (11-055 East Dr, off Hwy 62. From I-10, take Hwy 62 north approximately 11.5 miles to

Morongo Valley. Turn right on East Dr and head to the entrance of the preserve; 760/363-7190; www.bigmorongo.org.)

Horseback riding. Coyote Ridge Stables (50-639 Panorama Dr; 760/363-3380) offers guided trail rides through the foothills of Morongo Valley and the Big Morongo Preserve. Morning or evening rides are available, and the stables specialize in setting up private rides for small groups. The fee is $50 per person for a two-hour ride through the Big Morongo Preserve; advance reservations required.

YUCCA VALLEY

"Small, but really friendly"—that's how one resident describes the town of Yucca Valley. And it's quite true. Even on a red-hot summer day or in the midst of an afternoon thunderstorm, people in this high-desert town 30 miles northeast of Palm Springs are happy to chat about their community, which numbers around 18,000.

The so-called Old Town area on Twentynine Palms Highway, near the intersection of Pioneertown Road, has been revitalized, with spruced-up antique stores, gift shops, and a fine coffeehouse, the Water Canyon Coffee Co. (55-844 Twentynine Palms Hwy; 760/365-7771). Throughout the rest of the town, you'll find tack and feed stores, trading posts, specialty stores, and lots of realtors, since the clean country air and dramatic landscape draw more residents every year. And of course, there's the legendary Pioneertown, founded in 1946 as a Western movie set.

For more information, contact the Chamber of Commerce (55-569 Twentynine Palms Hwy; 760/365-6323; www.yucca valley.org).

ACTIVITIES

Golf. After first-time visitors have passed through the miles of high desert from Palm Springs into Yucca Valley, the well-tended golf course they see on the left comes as a bit of a surprise. The Blue Skies Country Club is a local treasure, with 18 holes, lots of mature trees, bent-grass greens, and year-round play at a reasonable fee. Golfers can choose to walk or rent a cart. There's a pro shop and a restaurant on the premises, and the course is known for being flat, scenic, and fairly forgiving. (55-100 Martinez Trail; from Hwy 62 go north on Camino Del Cielo to Martinez Trail; 760/365-0111.)

 Grubstake Days. This three-day celebration started in 1951 as a tribute to members of the California Mining Council, which was holding its annual meeting in Yucca Valley. The local Chamber of Commerce saw a great chance to recognize the early mining history of the area, as well as throw a good party, and the rest was history. Now held early each May, Grubstake Days is a favorite of locals throughout the region, who gather for a street fair, parade, carnival rides, pancake breakfast, 10K run, and monster-truck demos. Admission to the street fair and parade is free; other events have an admission or entry fee. For details, contact the Yucca Valley Chamber of Commerce (760/365-6323; www.yuccavalley.org).

Orchid farm. About 10 miles north of Yucca Valley, exotic orchids bloom en masse in the town of Landers. The Gubler Orchids greenhouses are home to dozens of species of these jungle flowers, which can be purchased on the premises or shipped throughout the country. Visitors are welcome to tour the growing facilities, which include some carniverous plants and bromeliads, to learn something about the art of orchid culture. The farm is open Monday to Saturday 10am to 4pm. (2200 Belfield Blvd, Landers. Take Hwy 62 to Old Woman Springs Rd north, go about 10 miles to Reche Rd and turn right, continue to Belfield Rd and go left to end of road; 760/364-2282 or 800/GUBLERS; www.gublers.com.)

 Visit Pioneertown. Up the road a piece from Yucca Valley, "PiTown" has a rich history that dates to the 1940s. This replica of a small Western town, complete with dusty unpaved streets and hitching posts, was originally built as a movie set. Constructed by a group of partners that included actors Russell Hayden, Gene Autry, and Roy Rogers, Pioneertown was the scene of dozens of Westerns filmed throughout the late '40s and '50s (remember *Cisco Kid*?). Although it's still used occasionally for shooting commercials, Pioneertown today is primarily a tourist attraction and tiny residential area, since the structures built to resemble old-time banks, jails, saloons, and a schoolhouse are actually private homes. Visitors are welcome to come snap photographs, visit the vintage bowling alley (which doubles as a pool hall, saloon, and social club), and watch weekly staged gunfights by costumed locals (shows on Sundays at 2:30pm, except during the winter holidays; call 760/365-4096).

Pappy and Harriet's Pioneer Palace is the main PiTown attraction, drawing a largely local crowd from Yucca Valley, Twentynine Palms, and Joshua Tree for beer, burgers (and other American fare), music, and camaraderie. The Palace brings in a great mix of humanity, says area resident Szu Wang. "It's like a Fellini movie— you get guys from the Marine base, family types, tourists, young hipsters who want to do some shooters and soak up some atmosphere." The rock band Cracker has performed here as well, to enthusiastic, standing-room-only crowds. A rustic, one-level adobe with a courtyard open to the stars, the Palace is open Thursday through Sunday. Hours are, in the affectionate words of one Yucca Valley resident, "weird." When we last checked they were 5 to 11pm Thursday, 10am to 1am Friday and Saturday, 10am to 11pm Sunday (53-688 Pioneer Town Rd; 760/365-5956).

Another local landmark is the Pioneertown Motel (760/365-4879), originally built in 1947 and operated by a local couple. It has 19 rooms for rent at a price that's as yesteryear as the setting: about $49 a night on weekends, under 40 bucks during the week. Find it just behind Pappy and Harriet's place.

Given the dirt streets of Pioneertown, it's easy to understand the sign posted at one resident's house: "If you're raisin' dust, you're drivin' too fast." Go slow, take some photos, and enjoy the local flavor and the surrounding views of boulder-covered hills, Joshua trees, and development-free open spaces. For more detailed stories about Pioneertown, check out the articles posted on www.pioneertown.com. To visit, take Interstate 10 to Highway 62 (Twentynine Palms Highway), go about 25 miles northeast to Yucca Valley. Turn left (north) on Pioneertown Road and drive about 4 miles to the sign that reads "Pioneertown 1946." The town lies to the right.

Starry Nights Festival. With its ink-black nights far from big cities, and local "dark-sky" laws that prevent light pollution, Yucca Valley is the perfect choice for the annual Starry Night Festival each October. Started a few years back, when the

Western Regional Astronomical League hosted their annual conference here, the event has now turned into a celebration for the whole community. The two-day fest attracts astronomers from throughout the country, who converge for lectures and two

RIMROCK RANCH

Beyond Pioneertown, the two-lane road undulates for miles through desolately beautiful high-desert landscapes. Tucked into the wilderness is a quiet refuge that's especially popular with writers and other artists: RimRock Ranch Cabins.

Built sometime in the 1940s as a homestead, RimRock Ranch is a hidden treasure whose location appears on few maps. It was purchased about 10 years ago by Szu Wang and her husband, Dusty Wakeman, as a weekend escape from the Los Angeles area. For several years, they loaned the extra cabins on the property to friends or relatives, then decided the place would make a perfect inn. Far from the main roads, with four individual cabins that feature kitchens and private courtyards, the secluded ranch has become a haven for creative types seeking peace or channeling the muse.

"We've carved out a little niche here," says Wang, a professional set decorator who has furnished each cabin with antiques, "found" items, and imagination. "We get writers who come up and never leave the ranch for a couple of weeks." Wang says screenwriters, authors, and composers are among the guests who savor the hiking trails (the ranch is adjacent to the Pipes Canyon Wilderness Preserve), the still nights, and the breathtaking sunrises. And their dogs can do the same: The ranch allows neutered, well-socialized canines to accompany their owners for a small extra fee.

Since it's far from grocery stores and restaurants (aside from the Pioneer Palace a few miles away), visitors generally bring plenty of supplies and cook all their meals. There's a two-night minimum stay, and all rooms are designated nonsmoking. Rates start at $105 for the smaller cottages; higher for the cabin known as J.D.'s House, which will house up to four and includes a fireplace. For information and directions, contact RimRock Ranch Cabins (PO Box 313, Pioneertown, CA 92268; 760/228-1297; info@rimrockranchcabins.com; www.rimrock ranchcabins.com).

nights of stargazing. The star parties, where astronomers can help you locate various planets and constellations, are free, but tickets are required for the conference events and lectures. Also, it's wise to book a hotel room well in advance if you're staying nearby. For tickets, sky-viewing locations, and other information, call Yucca Valley Community Services (760/369-7211).

 Hi-Desert Nature Museum. For a closer look at the high desert's cultural and natural history, visit this bright, inviting collection of permanent and temporary exhibitions. The museum, a great destination for families, has Native American artifacts, vintage gold mining equipment, dioramas featuring desert flora and fauna, a large gem and mineral collection, and a kids' activity corner. A special highlight is the minizoo of rescued desert creatures, which offers a close look at desert rats, tortoises, chuckwallas, several varieties of snakes, tarantulas, and some alarmingly large scorpions. A gift shop carries guidebooks, maps, local crafts, jewelry, even packages of native wildflower seeds. Open year-round, Tuesday to Sunday 10am to 5pm; free admission (with donations welcome). Look for the museum on the north side of Highway 62 at the Community Center Complex (57-116 Twentynine Palms Hwy; 760/369-7212).

Desert tortoise rescue. This charming labor of love is run by Yucca Valley resident Rae Packard, who takes in injured or sick tortoises, restores them to good health, and then adopts them out. It's hard to imagine anyone harming these peaceful vegetarians, but they're often hit by cars and have become an endangered species. They make quiet but fascinating pets. Visitors may call Packard (760/369-1235) to arrange a tour of the rescue facility, which is licensed by the California Department of Fish and Game. Adoptions are free to qualified homes.

The Integratron. It's no easy matter to describe the Integratron, one of the high desert's landmarks and a continuing source of legend and lore. Let's start with the facts: it's a 38-foot high, 50-foot diameter, nonmetallic structure designed by the late engineer George Van Tassel, who began building it in the mid-1950s. Van Tassel claimed that much of the inspiration for his building, which he created as a human cell rejuvenation machine, came during a visit by technology-sharing aliens from

For a donation of $15 to $35 per year, animal lovers can support one of the critters in the Hi-Desert Nature Museum's minizoo. These creatures, including endangered species such as the mountain king snake and desert tortoise, as well as more common kangaroo rats, geckos, skinks, and gopher snakes, were rescued because they were injured or imprinted by humans and cannot be returned to the wild. Fill out an adoption form at the museum in Yucca Valley or request one by email at hdnm@juno.com.

Venus. Van Tassel passed away in 1978, after spending close to two decades building the Integratron, but the dome remains, about 10 miles outside Yucca Valley, as a testament to his vision. These days the dome and the nearby Giant Rock boulder attract a spectrum of visitors, from the simply curious to dedicated UFO seekers and New Age devotees. The Integratron presents monthly open houses, as well as occasional musical events (the acoustics are awesome) and other activities. Call 760/364-3126 for details about hours, admission, and special events. To reach the building, take Interstate 10 east to Highway 62 and continue northeast to the town of Yucca Valley. In Yucca Valley, turn left at Highway 247, also known as Old Woman Springs Road, and continue 10 miles to Reche Road. Turn right, and go about 2 miles to Belfield Road. Turn left and drive about 1 mile to the intersection of Belfield and Linn Roads.

RESTAURANTS

WATER CANYON COFFEE CO. ☆

This corner coffeehouse with a patio out front has a lot more to offer than good latte and espresso. It's also one of the artistic centers and meeting spots in town, a place that's helping to fuel the Old Town rejuvenation. The tranquil blue and turquoise walls provide a feeling of calm and refuge, and there are plenty of couches, tables, and chairs in the spacious, two-level room for cozying up with a book or a good conversation. A shelf in the back holds an eclectic mix of "gently used" books for sale; this is also a good place to pick up fliers on upcoming events throughout the area. On Saturday and Sunday nights (and the occasional Friday), Water Canyon hosts live music in a variety of genres. Refreshments include a good selection of herbal teas, coffee drinks, microbrewed beers, and smoothies. Simple breakfast items such as egg bagels and burritos are served until noon; sandwiches, soups, and salads until about 4pm. Soup choices change daily but can include navy bean, tomato-lentil or vegetable stew; the sandwich lineup features turkey, tuna, or fresh veggies on your choice of breads. Internet access is available for about 10 cents per minute. *55-844 Twentynine Palms Hwy, Yucca Valley; 760/365-7771; $;*

AE, DC, DIS, MC, V; no checks; breakfast, lunch every day; beer and wine only; no reservations; at corner of Pioneertown Rd and Twentynine Palms Hwy.

JOSHUA TREE NATIONAL PARK

In Joshua Tree National Park, bordered by the Little San Bernardino Mountains to the southwest, and the Eagle and Coxcomb Mountains to the south and east, wind-smoothed boulders pile up like clusters of weird grapes. Rock climbers from around the world swarm here each winter, their chalked hands searching for fissures left by eons of harsh weather. Less acrobatic travelers seek out the park's boulder-garden trails, hike to hidden year-round ponds (known as "tanks" in desert parlance), and revel at the view of stunning wildflowers and—if you're very lucky—occasional rare desert tortoises nibbling the spring blooms.

Recently the park has seen increased visitor interest. Joshua Tree gained the added cachet of national park status in 1994 with the passage of the Desert Protection Act, and the popularity of rock climbing here has caused its legions of winter visitors to soar to the point that it can be difficult to find a campsite during the cooler season, November through May.

The Protection Act brought more to Joshua Tree than a new name. Wilderness acreage expanded to 630,000 acres, bringing the total park acreage to 794,000, or about 1,237 square miles (about the same size as Yosemite National Park). Despite its vastness, the park has a road system so simple and limited (about 100 paved miles connecting three main entry points) that you can drive it in a single day or less. Unfortunately, virtually all park visitors are on or near these few roads, especially in spring (March and April), when the wildflowers bloom.

Don't get the idea that Joshua Tree is a queue of cars, however. Its remote location and weather extremes will always assure some elbowroom, even along Park Boulevard where it skirts Wonderland of Rocks. Visitors must pay $10 per vehicle admission at one of three entry points: West Entrance Station near the town of Joshua Tree, North Entrance Station on Utah Trail near Twentynine Palms, and the Cottonwood Spring Visitor Center 22 miles east of Indio.

It's true: The band U2 named their 1987 album The Joshua Tree *after the famous trees in the national park. In some reviews of the album, critics postulated that the band was using the title and cover image of the desert to symbolize a world thirsty for compassion and humanity.*

Park fees valid for seven days are collected at the north entrance station near Twentynine Palms and the western entrance near Yucca Valley, as well as the Cottonwood and Indian Cove ranger stations. The charge is $10 per car; $5 per person entering on foot, bicycle, motorcycle, or bus. Annual passes to Joshua Tree are $15; Golden Eagle passes, qualifying holders to unlimited, free admission to all national parks for one year, are also available. For U.S. citizens 62 and older, the Golden Eagle passes are sold for a one-time fee of $10, entitling the holder to unlimited, lifetime access.

Whether it's your first or 50th visit to Joshua Tree National Park, a stop at any of the three visitor centers is always a good idea. Maps, brochures, videos, books, and field guides are sold at all visitor centers, which are staffed by park rangers and naturalists. Information is also available about the many ranger-led hikes and talks offered seasonally throughout the park.

At the north entrance half a mile south of Highway 62, Twentynine Palms is the site of the Oasis Visitor Center and Park Headquarters. Hours here are 8am to 3:30pm every day, except Christmas day. Visitor centers are also located at Black Rock Canyon Campground, 4 miles south of Highway 62 near the town of Joshua Tree, and at Cottonwood Spring, 7 miles north of Interstate 10 at the park's south entrance. Occasionally, staff shortages necessitate temporary closures.

The town of Joshua Tree itself lies near the west entrance to Joshua Tree National Park and is home to about 14,000 residents. As the gateway to one of the most magnificent parks in the country, the little town draws a varied tourist crowd, and features several businesses geared toward climbing, hiking, and camping. The population includes a large artistic component, with plenty of musicians, visual artists, writers, and other creative folk maintaining full- or part-time residences in Joshua Tree. One reason we've heard quite a lot: The sunsets are like nowhere else on earth.

ACTIVITIES

SHOPS *Coyote Corner.* This cool little shop at the corner of Highway 62 and Park Boulevard (the west entrance to Joshua Tree) is a fun place to stop and browse. The place feels like your great-granddad's general store updated for the 21st century.

Detailed topography maps and hiking handbooks mingle with incense, handmade pottery, and candles. One wall features carabiners and other climbing equipment, while another is devoted to CDs from local artists. An international clientele drawn by the universal lure of the desert frequents Coyote Corner, and you might well hear Italian, German, or French, as well as accents from throughout the United States. Several publications are available in various foreign languages as well. The shop is as much about socializing as shopping, so feel free to chat up the staffers and get the skinny on local artists, the music scene, favorite hiking trails, and just about anything else you might want to know about the area. The store is open every day (6535 Park, Joshua Tree; 760/366-9683).

Desert Queen Ranch Tours. Step back about 100 years with a trip to the isolated Desert Queen Ranch, named for a nearby gold mine. The property was owned by Bill Keys, a miner and homesteader who built a house on the property around 1917. The Ranch is now a fascinating ghost town–like ruin that showcases the incredible ingenuity and resourcefulness of Bill Keys as he and his wife, Frances, raised a family here in the early 1900s. Keys's house is still standing, along with a number of other buildings and remnants of the old mine.

Admittance is by advance reservation only (call 760/367-5555 for reservations or purchase tickets at the Oasis Visitor Center). Tickets may also be purchased at the ranch gate, on a space-available basis, 15 minutes before a tour. The narrated, 1½ hour tours are offered daily October to May and cost $5 for adults, $2.50 for kids. To get to the ranch, enter Hidden Valley Campground, keep to the right, turn left at the T-intersection, and follow the road approximately 2 miles to the locked gate. A ranger will meet you there.

Hi-Desert Playhouse. This volunteer-built community playhouse is home to plays and vaudeville acts, as well as the occasional experimental dance, music, or theater piece. In addition to the 175-seat theater with an art gallery in the lobby, there's an additional hall that hosts dance lessons, theater workshops, rehearsals, and other community events. Look for the distinctive red-and-white building marked "Hi-Desert Cultural

Center" at 61-231 Twentynine Palms Highway, Joshua Tree; box office: 760/366-3777.

Scenic drives. The main, paved road through Joshua Tree explores the transition between the Mojave and Colorado portions of the Great Sonoran Desert. You can drive the 65 miles from the town of Joshua Tree to Interstate 10, passing through Hidden Valley, Queens Valley, and Cottonwood Spring along the way.

A number of dirt roads are accessible from the main route, if you'd like to venture down the unbeaten path. Among them is Pinkham Canyon Road, which begins at Cottonwood Spring Visitor Center and connects to a service road next to Highway 10. This is a challenging, 20-mile drive along Smoke Tree Wash and Pinkham Canyon with sections running through soft sand and rocky floodplains. Only high-clearance, 4-wheel-drive vehicles should attempt this route.

Geology Tour Road turns south from the paved road 2 miles west of Jumbo Rocks. A route guide is available at the beginning

DESERT DRIVING

Whether you're driving an old banger or a new Benz, automobile travel in remote desert regions such as Joshua Tree can be potentially challenging and sometimes downright dangerous. Before you head for the desert, it's worth having your car serviced (pay special attention to radiator hoses and fan belts) to make sure it's in reliable condition. Be sure to let someone know about your trip plans: the route, destination, and return date. Let them know if you change your plans. Finally, since you won't find any gas stations inside the preserve, fill your tank before you leave the interstates, and keep an eye on the gauge and road map so you have enough fuel to make it to your next fill-up.

Always carry several gallons of drinking water per person (an extra few gallons for the car isn't a bad idea, either). In the event of a breakdown, stay with the car and wait for help—automobiles are easier to spot than people, and you'll want to stay close to your water supply. Don't venture off main routes unless you are an experienced desert wanderer, and even then don't travel alone—a companion car can be essential for of the road, as well as at all visitor centers, for the 17-mile round-trip through the unique geology of Pleasant Valley.

The Covington Flats area offers a look at some of the park's largest Joshua trees, as well as juniper and pinyon pine. Chuck O'Brien, a Joshua Tree resident (and a tribal ranger at the Indian Canyons near Palm Springs), says this is one of his favorite areas in the desert. "There are no tourists and it's all dirt road getting there. It's some of the prettiest area you've ever seen." To reach Covington Flats, take Highway 62 to the La Contenta exit (about 3 miles west of the town of Joshua Tree). After La Contenta turns into a dirt road, continue about 1.7 miles and bear left on the Covington Flats dirt road. Lower Covington Flat is about 5 miles past that.

Camping. The park is home to nine campgrounds: Belle, Black Rock, Cottonwood, Hidden Valley, Indian Cove, Jumbo Rocks, Ryan, Sheep Pass, and White Tank, at elevations from 3,000 to 4,500 feet. This is camping for hardy souls, by the way. Only Black Rock and Cottonwood have water available, and none of the campgrounds provide shade structures or RV

minor emergencies such as pulling you free from soft sand or going for help if your ride conks out. A buddy system isn't necessary in the more popular areas such as Joshua Tree, but it's smart to have a cell phone with you.

Best times to travel are in the shoulder season—late fall and spring, when temperatures are generally below 80°F. Winter weather means cool, usually clear days and freezing nights, and when a storm blows through, there can even be snow flurries. Be prepared with a warm jacket, pants, and hat, but dress in layers so you can peel down on sunny days. This is also true for spring, when the likelihood of 75°F-plus days is good, but nights are still cold and odd storms can surprise you. Spring means great weather and wildflowers, making it the most popular time to visit the the high desert. From April to October (or later), temperatures vault into the 90s and above. Your clothing strategy shifts to heat protection: wide-brimmed hats, lightweight shirts and pants, and sunblock. Drinking water at 15-minute intervals or less becomes critically important: Drink as much as 2 gallons a day if you're out and about in the heat.

hookups. Still, a night under skies so dark you'll probably see some constellations for the first time is just one of the rewards of staying here.

To make reservations, contact Joshua Tree National Park by phone (760/367-5500 or 800/365-2267), by mail (74-485 National Park Dr, Twentynine Palms, CA 92277), or via the national park reservations Web site (reservations.nps.gov) This site is particularly useful, since it gives specific directions to campsites and lists the amenities of each. You can also make reservations right on the Web site.

A 14-day limit applies to all campgrounds from October through May and a 30-day limit applies June through September. If you're arriving without a reservation, park rangers recommend showing up at the park at sunrise, then checking out the different campgrounds for space.

For those who really like to rough it, backcountry camping (away from the designated sites) is also allowed. Visitors must park at one of the campsites and register at the backcountry bulletin board, noting the time they'll be returning (this is a safety feature; campers who don't return will trigger a search party). All backcountry camping must be at least 1 mile away from the bulletin board and 500 feet off any roads.

No matter where you stay, there are some basic guidelines to follow as per the National Park Service:

Two cars, three tents, and up to six people are allowed for each family campsite. If you're going to have a campfire, bring your firewood; collecting wood or other plant materials is forbidden in the national park. If you're camping in an area without toilets or trash containers, be sure to bring plastic bags to take your trash when you leave. Please don't feed the local wildlife, such as coyotes and squirrels—if they lose their fear of humans and their ability to find food, it's bad news for the animals. And don't try to bury toilet paper. It never stays buried for long and wrecks the beauty of the desert like nothing else. Pack it out, preferably in Ziploc bags.

Visitors are also asked to respect the desert's magnificent silence with "quiet hours" in all campsites from 10pm to 6am. This includes generators and motors as well as loud music.

There are no hotel accommodations inside the park, nor can you buy food, gasoline, or any other supplies. You've heard it before, but we'll say it again: Be prepared. The desert is a beautiful but ruthless environment where you don't want to get stranded, hungry, or lost.

Finally, bring more water than you think you'll need. It's available at Oasis Visitor Center in Twentynine Palms (near the park's north entrance) and at Indian Cove Ranger Station. Remember: The only campsites with water are Black Rock and Cottonwood.

Here's a quick rundown on each site:

Belle Campground consists of 18 sites on a first-come, first-served basis at no charge. There is no water available at this campground, which may close during the summer when visitation decreases due to the heat. On Pinto Basin Road, 1.4 miles south of Pinto Way.

Black Rock Campground, open year-round but far from any climbing spots, is a large, popular site in the northwest corner of the park, with 100 sites, flush toilets, a dump station, and water. Site number 61 is wheelchair accessible. Reservations accepted; fee charged. At the end of Joshua Lane, 5 miles south of Highway 62 in Yucca Valley.

Cottonwood Campground is also open year-round with 62 individual and 3 group sites. Group site number 2 is wheelchair accessible. This campground is very close to the Pinkham Canyon bike trail and a number of great hikes. Water, flush toilets, and a dumping station are available. Reservations accepted; fee charged. Located near the Cottonwood Spring Visitor Center at the south entrance to the park.

Hidden Valley Campground is tucked into a beautiful valley surrounded by rock formations and is near Queen Valley bike routes. It's popular with rock climbers and can fill up quickly. Open year-round on a first-come, first-served basis, the 39 sites are provided at no fee. No water. On the main park road, 8.5 miles southeast of the west entrance.

Indian Cove Campground accepts reservations for the 107 individual and 13 group sites. There is no water at this year-round campground, which is far from any bike trails. Fee for group sites. At the end of Indian Cove Road, 2.7 miles south of Highway 62 between Joshua Tree and Twentynine Palms.

Jumbo Rocks Campground is surrounded by picturesque rock formations and boulders, has 129 sites available, first-come, first-served, and no water. Site number 11 is wheelchair accessible. There is no fee for this campground, which is open year-round. On the main park road, 2.5 miles southwest of Pinto Way.

Ryan Campground is also available on a first-come, first-served basis. There are 31 sites, all at no charge. This campground may be closed during the summer. This area fills up quickly on weekends. On the main park road, half a mile east of the intersection of Keys View Road.

Sheep Pass Campground, which offers just six group sites, is open year-round. A fee is charged, and reservations are required. This is the highest elevation campground in the park at 4,500 feet; no water. On main park road, 5.8 miles west of Pinto Way.

White Tank Campground, far from Hidden Valley, has some climbing nearby but is said to have poor quality rock. There are 15 sites, none with water. This campground is open year-round on a first-come, first-served basis at no charge. On Pinto Basin Road, 3 miles south of Pinto Way.

Camping, gourmet style. For all the joys of camping, without the pesky tent assembly and leaky air mattresses, call Galileo's: The Discovery Company. This trailer-tent outfitter specializes in "turn-key camping" at JT National Park—setting up a large or small tent trailer complete with beds, kitchen, and lounging area before you arrive. They'll also lay in plenty of firewood, and provide a home-style breakfast with muffins and cof-

SCIENCE CLASSES

Adult classes in campfire cooking, desert survival skills, birding, nature photography, and other region-related topics are offered through the Desert Institute at Joshua Tree National Park. The programs are held outdoors and last from one to three days (with participants staying overnight at campsites within the park). Presented in conjunction with the University of California, Riverside, several of the courses may be taken for college credit, and all are designed for those age 16 and over. For more information, contact the Desert Institute (760/367-5525; www.joshuatree.org/field.html).

fee the next day. You arrange to reserve the campsite through the Park Service, and Galileo's will do the rest. The company also rents bicycles and trailer-tents, and leads full- and half-day "bike & hikes" (61-762 Twentynine Palms Hwy; 760/366-0308; galileos @earthlink.net; www.galileos.org).

At the other end of the amenities spectrum, there's free camping available on the Bureau of Land Management Land around the park. It is dusty, however, with no water or toilets available. This is a viable alternative in the event you find park campgrounds full, although it is a bit of a drive. From the town of Joshua Tree, head east for 2 miles on Highway 62. Turn north on Sunfair Road, pass a small airport, and turn right (east) on Broadway about 2 miles north of Highway 62. Continue past where the road turns to dirt and another mile to some phone lines. Turn north/northeast here and follow any dirt road out to the large, dry lake bed. You are now on BLM land.

 Hiking. A wide variety of day hikes are yours for the trekking in Joshua Tree, from easy nature trails to strenuous, all-day adventures. The following is a small sample of trails the park has to offer. For a more extensive list, maps and guides are available at all visitor centers in the park. You can also order online at www.joshuatree.org, the Web site of the Joshua Tree National Park Association. The latter has an excellent selection of books specific to Joshua Tree, such as rock-climbing guides and books on local wildflowers.

Among the park's many leisurely nature trails is the **Cottonwood Spring Trail** loop (easy, 1 mile), along which signs interpret the plants and animals of the Colorado Desert. The trailhead is located at Cottonwood Spring campground parking area.

If seeing rare bighorn sheep and Native American petroglyphs sounds like fun, your best bet is the **Barker Dam Trail** loop (easy, 1.1 miles). Barker Dam, the location of a natural drainage where surface water gathers seasonally in a rocky basin, has long supported wildlife and drew the earliest human inhabitants of the area as well. Around the turn of the century, the natural water-storing capabilities of the basin were augmented by ranchers who grazed cattle in the high valleys in the western half of Joshua Tree. This "tank" was later enlarged in the 1950s, and the lake that now forms here is used by many species, including migratory water-

Given Joshua Tree's past as a mining area, it's not surprising that a number of abandoned mine shafts can be found in the park. Although they might be inviting, the entrances are generally surrounded with crumbling rock and rotten lumber supports that can conceal 100-foot drops. When it comes to old mines the Park Service says, "Stay out and stay alive."

fowl. Look for bedrock mortars created by the Indians for grinding seeds; panels of petroglyphs are also located along the route. To reach the trailhead, follow the main park road from Joshua Tree or Cottonwood Spring to the Hidden Valley Campground turnoff. Bear right at the fork in the campground road and follow the marked dirt road to the Barker Dam parking area, where you'll find the trailhead at the north end of the lot.

Mastodon Peak Trail (easy, 2.5 miles) is another loop hike that leads past the ruins of a mine and ore-processing mill near the base of Mastodon Peak, an oddly shaped block of fractured monzonite. Agile hikers not afraid of heights can scramble to the top of the peak for wonderful views of the surrounding area. The trailhead is located at Cottonwood Spring, a half mile past the campground entrance on the paved road leading southeast from the visitor center.

Hike through Joshua trees and junipers, oaks and pinyon pine along **Pine City Trail** (easy, 3 miles round-trip). Watch for this area's many species of wildlife, as well as views of the snowcapped San Gorgonio Mountains. The trailhead is at the end of a dirt road north of the main park route opposite Geology Tour Road, 5 miles west of Pinto Way.

For a much longer and a bit tougher trek, check out **Lost Palms Oasis Trail** (moderate, 7.4 miles round-trip), which shares a trailhead with Mastodon Peak Trail at Cottonwood Spring. The springs located in Lost Palms Canyon are a rare haven for a variety of plants and animals and are another water source frequently visited by the elusive bighorn sheep. Planted by miners, the cottonwood trees and fan palms create some valuable shady spots for a breather before you return via the same route.

To take a look at Joshua Tree National Park's best-preserved mining operations, not to mention some great views, follow the old wagon road that is now **Lost Horse Mine Trail** (moderate, 4 miles round-trip) to the foundations of old buildings, settling tanks, cast-iron machinery, mine shafts, and a stamp mill on the slope of Lost Horse Mountain. The trailhead is located at a parking lot at the end of a dirt road that leads southeast from Keys View Road, 2.5 miles south of its junction with the main park road.

The **Ryan Mountain Loop Trail** (moderate, 9.75 miles) begins at Ryan Campground and completely encircles Ryan Mountain, joining the California Riding and Hiking Trail near mile 14. This hike provides a nice perspective on Lost Horse Valley.

Although the route is rocky and steep, it's only 1.5 miles to the summit of Ryan Mountain, and the trail is in good condition. **Ryan Mountain Trail** (strenuous, 3 miles round-trip) leads to a breathtaking, 360-degree view of Joshua Tree National Park. The trailhead is marked by a large sign at a parking area on the south side of the park road, 1 mile west of the entrance to Sheep Pass Campground.

The trail to **Warren Peak** (strenuous, 5 miles round-trip) takes you through a thick stand of large Joshua trees in Black Rock Canyon, which is cooler and wetter than most of the park. At the summit, take in the scenic vistas in all directions before returning the way you came. The trail is faint and hard to follow in places, but the general route is clear. The trailhead is at the south end of Black Rock Campground, although there is no parking at the trailhead itself; leave your vehicle at the Black Rock Visitor Center and walk to the edge of the campground.

Wonderland Connection Trail (strenuous, 11 miles round-trip) follows a rocky wash that usually contains some water through the valley of Oh-bay-yo-yo, which has small boulder caves. This route contains rugged terrain and boulders that require scrambling around, over, or under and should be attempted only by those who are proficient at bouldering. This trail begins at the Keys west backcountry board.

Rock climbing. With its countless towering cliffs of cracked and weathered stone and more than 4,000 charted climbing routes on high-angled faces, flared chimneys, and difficult jam cracks, Joshua Tree National Park draws rock climbers from all over the planet. Because many of the routes are short, it is possible to tackle a number of them in one day. The climbs are generally steeper and feature better rock on the eastern sides of formations. Popular routes are found in Wonderland of Rocks, Indian Cove, Hidden Valley, and the Lost Horse area. For "peak baggers," the park has 10 mountains over 5,000 feet in elevation.

Given the fact that more than 1 million visitors come to the park each year—many of them strictly for rock climbing—the use of fixed anchors, such as expansion bolts, has prompted the

National Park Service to evaluate the compatibility of such fixtures with wilderness values. Since 1993, Joshua Tree has prohibited new bolts and replacement of existing bolts until this issue is decided. Heavy use of the easily accessible climbing areas has resulted in multiple short trails and damaged resources at the bases. The park asks your cooperation in sticking to existing routes and packing out whatever you carry in.

In addition to reference books on rock climbing that can be purchased at park visitor centers, several good climbing guides are available, including *Joshua Tree Sports Climbs*, with over 250 clip-and-go routes with maps and topography, and *Joshua Tree Bouldering*. Both guidebooks can be ordered through the Adventurous Travel Bookstore at www.gorp.com.

Rock climbing classes. Climbers of every level can hone their skills with the Joshua Tree Rock Climbing School. Classes are offered year-round except July and August, and can range from several hours to several days. A basic climbing class is offered each Saturday during the season; here, beginners learn the nuts and bolts of knots, belaying, rappelling, and rope-protected climbing. For a complete list of classes and seminars, contact the climbing school (760/366-4745 or 800/890-4745; www.desertgold.com).

Vertical Adventures, Inc., is another comprehensive rock climbing school with operations in Joshua Tree from September through May. One-day classes for beginners and intermediate climbers are offered in addition to advanced seminars on leading climbs and rescue techniques. Individual instruction available by appointment. For a complete list of classes and seminars, contact the climbing school (800/514-8785; BGvertical@aol.com; www.vertical-adventures.com).

Wildlife. Don't let the seemingly harsh and quiet desert environment fool you. Life is plentiful in Joshua Tree National Park well beyond its namesake vegetation, cacti, and wildflowers. Darting among the rocks, trees, and bushes are numerous cottontail, kangaroo rats, chipmunks, and black-tailed antelope squirrels, to name only a few of the smaller mammals. Among the larger of the area's more than 350 vertebrate species are mule deer and mountain lion, as well as the elusive bobcat and bighorn sheep. There are two species of fox within the park, and

KILLER BEES?

Call it a bad remake of The Sting: *A bee attack was reported on June 25, 2000, at Joshua Tree National Park. Four men were hiking in the park near mile marker number 22 on the main park road when they were swarmed and stung repeatedly by bees. While running back to the vehicle, one of the hikers also suffered a broken leg. The four ended up at the High Desert Medical Center for treatment, and while the episode hasn't been repeated, visitors are now urged to be more cautious. Another attack was reported in Twentynine Palms a few months later. Park Superintendant Ernest Quintana notes that in picnic areas and campgrounds, food and soft drinks can attract bees and shouldn't be left unattended. Bees are also drawn to the water that drips from car air conditioners, so be careful when returning to your car.*

coyotes are plentiful. While normally shy, coyotes can become quite bold when habituated to humans. Be sure to store all food securely and never offer handouts or leave small pets—sometimes seen as "snacks" by coyotes—unattended.

Joshua Tree is home to a number of federally listed endangered and threatened species. The park's population of the Mojave's threatened desert tortoise is estimated at approximately 12,700 animals, most often found in the Pinto Basin but ranging throughout the park. A 90 percent decline in this docile reptile's numbers has taken place over the last 50 years, primarily due to loss of habitat. In addition, off-road traffic has often crushed the tortoises, which hide from the vehicles in their underground burrows. If you see one of these slow-moving creatures, observe from a distance and handle only when necessary to remove it from a road or other danger. Special forms are available at visitor centers for reporting sightings, which are helpful to park rangers.

Of Joshua Tree's myriad invertebrates, two are poisonous spiders—the black widow and brown recluse. However, the tarantulas and scorpions found in the park are nonpoisonous, though it's said their bites do feel much like bee stings. Though bites are uncommon, it pays to be cautious when hiking or climbing in the warmer months, when rattlesnakes often bask in the morning sun, then retreat to the shade of boulders, mine shafts, and holes during the hottest part of the day. A good rule of thumb is never to stick your hands or feet anywhere you can't see.

Bird-watching. Bird-watchers will have plenty to see in Joshua Tree, with approximately 60 species nesting within the park and hundreds more passing through during their spring or fall migrations. Gambel's quail are commonly seen, as are scrub jays, red-tailed hawks, three types of owls, and a variety of hummingbirds. On the other end of the spectrum, you may be lucky enough to spot an endangered peregrine falcon or a bald eagle, a federally designated threatened species.

Top birding months are April and May, then once again during the fall. In addition to seeing migratory birds during these seasons, there's also more likelihood of finding the native birds more active and visible than during the searing summer months. For those with a particular interest in birding, a checklist can be purchased at the visitor centers.

Wildflower viewing. Given the rather stark landscape of the desert, it's no surprise that the spring wildflower season is anticipated by locals and tourists alike. Seeing the browns and grays of the hillsides carpeted with brilliant annuals like dandelions, wooly marigolds, and desert sunflowers is a treat indeed, as is seeing the Joshua trees and other yuccas in full flower. Plants don't bloom all at once, so the season can vary from as early as February through May. The previous year's rainfall and the spring temperatures also affect this natural flower show.

Call the main park number (760/367-5500) in late winter and spring for information on current conditions. There's also a wildflower hotline (760/340-0435) during the blooming season where you can get specific location and species information.

Mountain biking. Though climbing and bouldering are by far the most popular activities in Joshua Tree, cycling is gaining in popularity. While the park is planning to open 29 additional miles of bike trails, these haven't been completely mapped or marked yet. In the meantime, cyclists can stick to paved or unpaved roads and marked trails; no cross-country riding is permitted. Some routes are suitable for beginning cyclists, while others are rigorous and demanding; detailed directions for all bike routes are available at all visitor centers. Note: It's always smart to check with park rangers regarding road conditions before you go.

A park-designated mountain bike route, **Queen Valley** (easy, 12 miles round-trip) is a flat, occasionally washboarded dirt road from the day-use area at the intersection of Geology Tour Road and Park Boulevard to Hidden Valley Campground. (Note: Park Boulevard, the main park road, is also somewhat confusingly called Quail Springs, as well as a combination of Park Routes 11 and 12.) From the parking lot at the day-use area, you'll head north across Park Boulevard through a desert landscape for a mile to a hairpin intersection, where the bike route turns left. (Going straight ahead leads you to the backcountry "board" for hikers heading to Desert Queen Mine and Pine City.) As you continue riding, you'll pass a trailhead to Wonderland Ranch, where you can park and lock your bike and take a short walk through monzogranite mounds and structures. Farther along the bike route, you'll have the opportunity to dismount again and hike to Barker Dam (see Hiking, above). When you reach Hidden Valley, you can check out the 1-mile nature trail loop and watch climbers on sheer granite cliffs before pedaling 6 miles back to where you started.

Beginning from the same point as the Queen Valley route (above), **Geology Tour Road** (easy/moderate, 5.4 miles each way to Squaw Tank, plus 6.1-mile loop through Pleasant Valley) is a great mountain bike route for observing the geology of the park. The *Geology Tour Road Guide* is available for 25 cents at visitor centers and sometimes at the trailhead. Numbered trail markers correspond to numbers in the guide. The road is a bit bumpy through the Pleasant Valley section and is, therefore, designated for 4-wheel-drive vehicles.

To travel by mountain bike from the Colorado Desert to the Mojave and back, ride **Pinkham Canyon Road** (strenuous, 23.8 miles round-trip) and observe washes, cholla cactus, canyons, and abundant wildlife. The route begins at Cottonwood Spring Visitor Center and leads you through the transitional zone between two ecosystems to Snow Cloud Mine. There, you have the options of returning the way you came (for a total of 23.8 miles), continuing in the same direction into the Cottonwood Mountains and looping back through Pinkham Canyon (totaling 36.7 miles), or circling back to the starting point through Thermal Canyon (for a total of 39.4 miles).

Need mountain bike repairs, supplies, or even a brand-new bike? Head for the Bike Business, a shop in Yucca Valley that is open every day year-round (56-778 Twentynine Palms Hwy, Yucca Valley; 760/365-1078).

Two other bike outfitters are located in Indio: Don's Bike Shop (81-582 Hwy 111; 760/347-0119) and Luis's Bicycle Shop (82-493 Hwy 111; 760/775-4055).

Horseback riding. For both equestrians and hikers, the California Riding and Hiking Trail runs 37 miles through the park and a wide range of vegetation, including pinyon and juniper forests and creosote-dominated lowlands. The western terminus is off Joshua Lane near Black Rock Canyon, and the eastern trailhead is off Utah Trail at the park boundary. Intermediate access points are located at Covington Flats, Keys View, and Geology Tour Roads. Camping with horses is allowed at Black Rock Horse Camp off Joshua Lane ($10 per night, water available) and Ryan Horse Camp (free, no water available). Both camps are near the California Riding and Hiking Trail. Supplies, including feed and tack, are available in Yucca Valley.

RESTAURANTS

CROSSROADS CAFE ★★

Marked by a row of international flags, this inviting little restaurant is a hub of Joshua Tree activity. In turns a dining room, bar, conversational salon, music venue, meeting place, art gallery, and hangout, the Crossroads is a regional treasure. Locals and tourists alike drop in to get caught up on local news, listen to music (folk, jazz, blues, and more), recharge over a cup of good cappuccino or microbrewed beer, gossip, and, of course, enjoy the fresh, well-priced food. Morning foods include a decadent French toast made with challah bread and stuffed with raspberry cream cheese, as well as simpler offerings like buckwheat pancakes and granola/fruit sundaes. For lunch and dinner, standouts are the grilled portobello mushroom sandwich dressed with pesto, whopper-size burgers cooked to order, the Grilled Coyote (actually, a tasty marinated grilled chicken breast), the entree-size Harvest Salad, and various daily specials.

Soup or salad is included with most of the entrees (including sandwiches), so if you're on a tight budget you could split something and still come out satisfied. The place is both rustic and artsy, with a lovely sunset sky painted on the ceiling, and comfortable old tables, chairs, and sofas. Beverages include bracing espresso drinks, smoothies (a special blessing during summer months), soft drinks, juices, and a big selection of boutique-style beers. Paintings and photographs on the walls were created by local artists, and most are for sale. In addition to the air-conditioned interior, there's a shaded patio with a handful of tables. *61-715 Twentynine Palms Hwy, Joshua Tree; 760/366-5414; $; cash only; breakfast, lunch, dinner every day (check with the restaurant for seasonal or holiday closures); beer and wine only; no reservations; on Hwy 62 west of Park Blvd.*

TWENTYNINE PALMS

The last town on Highway 62 before the road plunges eastward across empty desert, Twentynine Palms is best known as the base for the Marine Corps Air Ground Combat Center and is the easternmost gateway to Joshua Tree National Park. It's here that you'll find the park's Oasis Visitors Center (74-485 National Park Dr, corner of Utah Trail before you enter the park; 760/367-5500), which received all-new interpretive exhibits in late 1999. Because Joshua Tree is often the first national park many visitors see as they begin a trip through the Southwest from Los Angeles, Oasis Visitors Center now has a "gateway" interactive exhibit that introduces Grand Canyon, Bryce Canyon, Zion, and other Southwestern parks.

While in Twentynine Palms, keep an eye out for the town's ever-increasing number of wall-scale outdoor murals, each featuring a historic moment from the area's past. Lovers of desert paintings should stop at the Twentynine Palms Artists Guild Art Gallery (74-055 Cottonwood Dr; 760/367-7819), located next door to Twentynine Palms Inn.

LODGINGS

BEST WESTERN GARDENS INN & SUITES ★

Set against the boulder-strewn mountains of Joshua Tree National Park, this fairly standard motor inn is by far the nicest chain-affiliated lodging near the park's eastern entrance. Everyone from military individuals and families on business at the nearby base to national park visitors and many foreign tourists (especially from Germany) stays here. Its location lends travelers a great sense of "being there" in a desert landscape, even though it's plunked on the same long stretch of Highway 62 that's scattered with an anonymous collection of minimalls, gas marts, and other encrustations doing their best to spoil a designated California State Scenic Highway. Organized around a good-size swimming pool (heated year-round), the dusky-colored inn lines up 84 rooms in one- and two-story buildings. Twelve suites have efficiency kitchens for whipping together a simple meal after a day spent exploring Joshua Tree. The nicely furnished king-bed suites (some with murals of desert scenes) also have queen-size sofa beds, while one two-room suite and two minisuites include hot tubs. Ask for a room with a view of the mountains to the south, and do make a point of dropping into the outdoor Jacuzzi, which is great for evening star-watching. The complimentary continental breakfast includes pastries, locally baked bread, and a full range of cereals, fruit, juices, and coffee. *71-487 Twentynine Palms Hwy, Twentynine Palms; 760/367-9141 or 800/528-1234; $$; AE, DC, DIS, MC, V; no checks; www.bestwestern.com; at west end of town.* &

ROUGHLEY MANOR BED & BREAKFAST INN ★★

In 1924 desert pioneers Elizabeth and Bill Campbell turned a once-primitive campsite next to a hand-dug well into an elegant two-story, stone-walled mansion. Today, a rustling oasis of mature fan palms, rose gardens, and trickling fountains surrounds the product of their years of toil. Located near the northeast edge of what is now Joshua Tree National Park, Roughley Manor has aged well (as stone is wont to do), and innkeepers Jan and Gary Peters couldn't be a better fit to carry on the original owners' dream. The two-story main house has a "great room" downstairs—a huge living room almost entirely paneled and trimmed with hardwood wainscoting and moldings. The grandest accommodations are the Campbell and Magnolia Rooms upstairs, each with fireplace and four-poster or canopy bed, and deep-set windows that look out into the treetops and surrounding desert landscape. There are five rooms in the stone main house and two in the stone "museum house," plus a wood-frame cottage and a small farmhouse. All are air-conditioned. Jan Peters's interior designs are tasteful, classical New England, with a merciful lack of stuffed bears and knickknacks. Her husband, Gary, seems never without a project, and the place is immaculate right down to the raked sandy yard (no lawns) with its comfortable, upholstered outdoor furniture set in the shade. Guests get a hearty breakfast of fresh fruit, toast, and twice-baked potatoes topped with eggs, bacon, and cheese (among other menus). The Peterses also set out desserts, coffee, and tea each evening. Evenings here are perfect for a soak in the hot tub under a sky peppered with stars. *74-744 Joe Davis Rd, Twentynine Palms; 760/367-3238; $–$$; MC, V; checks OK; themanor@cci-29palms.com; www.virtual29.com/themanor; take Utah Trail off Hwy 62 north to Joe Davis Rd.*

TWENTYNINE PALMS INN ★★

Rustic, sparsely landscaped, and with dirt roads between the bungalows, the Inn captures the essence of an old-time California desert stay. This historic cluster of cottages, which sprawls over 35 acres, has been operated by the same family since 1928. It's the quintessential hideaway for stressed-out film industry types, European travelers, lizard-skinned desert oldsters, and just about everyone else. Built beside the Oasis of Mara, a rare natural source of open water in the high desert, the Inn offers bungalow rooms in the 1929 "old Adobe" section with sun patios (great for nude sunbathing) and fireplaces. Wood-frame cottages Gold Park and Faultline were moved here in 1928. Larger lodgings include several houses and cabins; well-known local painter Irene Charlton occupied one, La Querencia, for many years, and her artwork now decorates the walls. Interiors are rustic yet comfortable, with swamp coolers (rather than colder, but more humid air conditioners) keeping them reasonably comfortable in summer. Bird-watching, swimming, and tours of the Inn's large organic vegetable garden are the major activities here. Many guests tour nearby Joshua Tree National Park (no lodging is located closer to the park), or just hunker down in the 100°F-plus heat if they visit in summer. Adjacent to the pool, the restaurant serves the best meals in the area. All seasonal vegetables come from the inn's year-round garden. The menu favors a hearty continental approach to grilled steaks, seafood, and chicken, and the bar blends up some of the best margaritas this side of Palm Springs. *73-950 Inn Ave, Twentynine Palms; 760/367-3505; $–$$; AE, DC, DIS, MC, V; checks OK; info@29palmsinn.com; www.29palmsinn.com; off National Park Dr, about a quarter mile to Inn Ave.* &

IDYLLWILD

IDYLLWILD

Gateway to San Jacinto State Park, this small resort town fills up each weekend with flatlanders who want a breath of crisp alpine air, a whiff of pines, a stay in a homey bed-and-breakfast, and perhaps a day hike or overnight backpacking trip into the wilderness. Snuggled into the San Jacinto Mountains at an altitude of 5,300 feet, the village is dominated by views of Tahquitz Rock (also known as Lily Rock) and Suicide Rock, both enormous draws for climbers, sightseers, and photographers.

Tourists may abound in Idyllwild, but nature is always within close reach. During the day, outsize gray squirrels scramble across rooftops, startling visitors with a chatter that resembles a rusty door hinge. Above, mountain blue jays call and respond like jazz musicians trading riffs, accompanied by the syncopation of woodpeckers and the high-pitched screech of circling hawks.

It's easy to tell the visitors from the locals: the tourists are the ones looking longingly at the windows of real estate offices, gazing at photos of cabins for sale, and figuring the price of a second mortgage in their heads. Houses up here run the gamut from humble one-bedroom abodes to breathtaking log-and-glass mansions beyond gated driveways. One thing is certain: The town has done a good job of maintaining its rustic flavor through the years. This is one place that you won't find tacky condos piled one upon another in a desperate scramble for a piece of the dream. In fact, a number of celebrities have discovered Idyllwild as a place to escape the crowds; longtime resident Marsha Bronson cites Brad Pitt, Nicolas Cage, and Michelle Phillips as just a few of the famous faces she's seen around town.

Idyllwild can get crowded during high season, which ranges roughly from April to late September, and then again at Thanksgiving and Christmas. If you're visiting on a weekend or during a holiday period, be sure to book accommodations several weeks in advance. Also, be aware that many inns require a minimum stay of two days on weekends. Midweek, it's generally no problem staying just one night, and many properties offer a discount Sunday through Thursday evenings.

In town, you'll find numerous small curio and gift shops oriented to the tourist trade, as well as several art galleries, restaurants (mostly ultracasual), some small grocery stores, and even a movie theater (more on this later).

Motorists reach the San Jacinto Mountains and the Idyllwild resort area by going east from Interstate 15 on Highway 74 through Hemet to Highway 243 and the final tortuously curved climb into the pines (total distance about 40 miles). You can also reach Idyllwild from Interstate 10: at Banning, take Highway 243 south about 25 miles into the heart of the mountains. Idyllwild is a popular destination for the members of various car clubs, by the way, who love to test their Alpine driving skills on the continuous S-curves through the mountains.

"Almost All the News—Part of the Time." That's the motto of the local newspaper, the weekly Idyllwild Town Crier, which began in 1946 as a six-page, mimeographed newsletter created by Ernest and Betty Maxwell.

For help with trip planning and other details, contact the Idyllwild Chamber of Commerce (54-295 Village Center Dr, downstairs from the *Idyllwild Town Crier*; 888/659-3259; www.idyllwild.org). It's smart to stop here to pick up a local map as well; for first-time visitors, Idyllwild's circle of streets in the downtown area can be confusing. For backcountry permits and information, stop in at the Idyllwild Ranger Station (San Jacinto Ranger District; 909/659-2117; at the corner of Hwy 243 and Upper Pine Crest Ave in the village).

ACTIVITIES

Hiking. Idyllwild is a superb destination for hikers, from day-trippers seeking an easy walk of an hour or two to serious backpackers who come for challenging trails and rock-climbing opportunities.

Both a hiking permit (which is free) and a parking pass known as the Adventure Pass ($5, which covers all occupants of the vehicle) are required to use most trails. Both are available at the ranger station at the address above. If you prefer, you may purchase an annual Adventure Pass for $30 ($15 for seniors), a considerable savings over the one-day passes if you plan to visit the area often. It's a good deal, since the pass is good not only for the San Bernardino National Forest around Idyllwild, but for the Cleveland, Los Padres, and Angeles forests as well.

The Adventure Pass is also sold at several local stores (just look for the signs advertising the passes). Note: Bicyclists and sightseers "just driving through" without parking needn't buy an Adventure Pass.

WATCH FOR BEARS

Although bears aren't roaming the streets of downtown Idyll-wild, the California Department of Fish and Game would like people to know how to deal with them. With an estimated population of perhaps 24,000 bears in the state, we're happy to have this information.

Rule 1: Avoidance is good. Most bears would prefer to spend as little time with people as possible (although they're terribly fond of people's foodstuffs, garbage, pet food, dirty dishes, and so on). Whether you're staying in a cabin or camping in a tent, keep your living area clean: Don't leave food lying around, keep barbecue grills scrubbed, and store food and garbage in bear-proof containers. Oh, and don't feed the bears; it encourages them to lose their natural fear of human beings. If you're camping and can't store supplies in the trunk of your car or securely inside your cottage, suspend food in a tree at least 10 feet above the ground, at least 4 feet away from the trunk, and on a slender branch that's under 4 inches thick. Make sure the tree's a fair distance away from sleeping areas, too.

Rule 2: If you encounter a bear, give it plenty of room to get away from you. Don't run; fleeing simply gives bears an excuse to give chase. If a bear decides to approach you, make a commotion with whatever you have at hand. Bear attacks are extremely rare, but if the unthinkable happens, rangers advise fighting back with rocks, branches, tent poles, and the like. Be sure to keep pets and children supervised whenever you're in bear country, and teach kids what to do if they run into a bear that's not named Smokey.

The ranger station also has a number of free maps and brochures about the area, as well as books for sale about regional hiking and climbing, native wildlife, birding guides, and more. Rangers we've talked to are happy to explain exactly where to find a trailhead or what kind of terrain to expect. Check with these local experts to find out everything from the latest weather forecast and up-to-date fire regulations to whether any bears have been spotted at local campgrounds.

Be sure to get a comprehensive list of trails at the ranger station. For a taste of what's in store, here are just a few of the routes:

The **Ernie Maxwell Scenic Trail** (easy, 2.6 miles) travels from Humber Park to the South Ridge Trail and has been a favorite jaunt since the late 1950s, when it was often used by equestrians and pedestrians to avoid traffic in town. The trail is named in honor of longtime resident Ernie Maxwell, who was instrumental in its construction. The trailhead can be found on Fern Valley Road, just before Humber Park.

Cedar Spring Trail (moderate, 6.5 miles round-trip) travels through private property, so be sure to respect private property rights and stay on the dirt road. The trail begins at 5,760 feet and connects with the Pacific Crest Trail, along the Desert Divide, south of Palm View Peak at 6,400 feet. The scenic Desert Divide offers views of the dry desert valley to one side, and green forests, lush from abundant rainfall, to the other side. To reach Cedar Spring, take the branch trail off the Pacific Crest Trail northeast for 1 mile. To reach the trailhead, follow Morris Ranch Road in Garner Valley to the trailhead sign.

Spectacular views are the hallmark of **South Ridge Trail** (moderate, about 3.6 miles one-way), which begins at an elevation of 6,800 feet and ascends 2,000 more to Tahquitz Peak Lookout. The route goes uphill along a scenic ridge, first through Jeffrey pine, live oak, and fir, then past thickets of lodgepole pines. The views from the trail and peak include the Desert Divide, Strawberry Valley, and beyond. Hike this one early in the morning to beat the summer heat. To reach the trailhead, drive south of Idyllwild and take Saunders Meadow Road. When you reach Pine Drive, turn left (north) for two blocks, then right (east) on Tahquitz Drive, and then right again on South Ridge Trail and Forest Access Road 5S11 and continue for 1.5 miles to the trailhead. Note: This trail, part of the San Jacinto Wilderness area, requires a permit.

Experienced hikers like the **Spitler Peak Trail** (difficult, 5 miles one-way), which visits the rarely used southern end of the San Jacinto Wilderness for some great views of the Mojave Desert from the Desert Divide. The hike starts in oak woodland and chaparral, then climbs to Jeffrey pine and Coulter pine trees. The trail gets steeper over the last mile before the divide and then climbs by switchbacks to the Pacific Crest Trail. The PCT follows the rocky ridgeline north and south. To reach the trailhead, take Highway 243 from Idyllwild to Mountain Center, at the intersection of

Highway 243 and Highway 74. Turn left (southeast) on Highway 74 to Apple Canyon Road and then turn left again. Continue on Apple Canyon Road to reach the trailhead parking.

The **Deer Springs Trail** (moderate, about 1 mile) leads from Highway 243 a mile north of Idyllwild to San Jacinto Peak. A shorter walk leads from the trailhead at Highway 243 to the top of Suicide Rock. Wilderness permit required.

Devil's Slide (moderate, about 5 miles) trail ascends from Humber Park to Saddle Junction, a gain of about 1,700 feet. From Saddle Junction, you can continue on to San Jacinto Peak, the Palm Springs Tramway, or Tahquitz Peak Lookout. Wilderness permit required; permits are limited for this particular route on weekends and holidays during the summer because of heavy use.

Rock climbing. Idyllwild is nirvana for climbers, especially during the summer months when Joshua Tree in the high desert is too hot to handle. The mountain community is home to two famous climbs: Suicide Rock, featuring more than 200 routes, and Tahquitz Rock (a.k.a. Lily Rock), with more than 100 routes. Both of these dramatic granite faces are within a half-hour hike of Humber Park (take N Circle Dr to Fern Valley Rd to the park).

For information on rock climbing instruction and guide services, drop by Nomad Ventures (54-415 N Circle Dr; 909/659-4853). You can also get maps and information from the ranger station in town. On the Web, you can find numerous personal sites that describe the exact routes and conditions of various climbs.

During the summer months (June through August), Vertical Adventures, Inc., closes its Joshua Tree operations and concentrates on classes and guided climbs in Idyllwild. Locations include Suicide Rock and Tahquitz Rock (at 1,000 feet high, it's the tallest climbing cliff in Southern California). Basic rock climbing class, $90; four-day rockcraft seminar, $345. Guided climbing and private instruction by appointment (800/514-8785; Bgvertical@aol.com; www.vertical-adventures.com).

In July and August, Joshua Tree Rock Climbing School also offers programs in Idyllwild. Classes can range from several hours to several days. For a complete list of classes and seminars, contact the climbing school (760/366-4745 or 800/890-4745; www.desertgold.com).

Camping. Hurkey Creek County Park is a spacious campground that's often solidly booked all summer long. The ranger here says it's also a favorite destination at Thanksgiving, when a number of families come up and roast their holiday turkeys on the grill. One hundred campsites are available, all with a limit of six people and two vehicles; fee required. Some rules to be aware of: No wood collecting within the park; dogs must be on a leash at all times; fires only in fire rings; quiet hours 10pm to 6am (no radios, generators, etc.). 56-375 Highway 74, about 4 miles southeast of Mountain Center off Highway 74; 909/659-2050.

GROUND SQUIRRELS

Although they're cute, ground squirrels should be avoided. They can carry diseases harmful to people, including bubonic plague (the notorious "Black Death" of the Middle Ages). The disease is transmitted from ground squirrels to humans (and their pets) via fleas, or through direct contact with sick or dead squirrels.

Campgrounds are regularly checked for the presence of plague-infected rodents and are closed for pest control if plague is detected. Although it's unlikely that anyone's going to contract bubonic plague during a visit to the mountains, rangers and health workers emphasize the following common-sense precautions:

1. Don't camp, sleep, or rest near animal burrows.

2. Don't touch or feed rodents such as ground squirrels, or store food and other supplies where they can access it. Don't touch ill or dead rodents.

3. Leave pets at home, if possible, or keep dogs leashed. Don't let dogs approach sick or dead squirrels, or explore any burrows. Protect pets with antiflea products.

4. If you or a pet become ill within a week of spending time in a possibly infected environment, call a physician or veterinarian immediately. Plague is treatable but must be caught early.

Lake Hemet Campground is a perfect spot for those who'd like a little bit of quality fishing time along with their camping experience. The narrow, 2-mile-long Lake Hemet is stocked every two weeks with trout (year-round, except December and January). In addition to trout, anglers here catch bluegill, catfish, and bass. Fishing is allowed from shore or by boat, with 12-foot aluminum boats for rent. Locals say the place to look for big fish is by the dam, where anglers occasionally reel in 20-pound catfish; oft-used baits include nightcrawlers, mealworms, Power Bait, and good old-fashioned cheese. This scenic lake is situated in a meadow surrounded by forests. Note: No swimming or wading allowed; no canoes, kayaks, sailboats, or inflatables. Fee for both day use and camping; picnic facilities. Off Highway 74 about 4 miles southeast of Mountain Center; 800/234-PARK.

For those lucky folk with their own horses, the **McCall Equestrian Park** makes a great home base for trail rides throughout the area. The facility is open year-round for horse camping exclusively, and has 55 wood or pipe paddocks available. Flush toilets and showers are among the amenities, but note that the water is turned off here during the winter, from November to April. The rate is $15 per night per rig (a truck and trailer, or a motorhome), and space is on a first-come, first-served basis. 28-500 McCall Park Road, one mile west of Mountain Center; 909/659-2311.

Mount San Jacinto State Park operates two campgrounds. The state campground in Idyllwild, just off Highway 243 near Pine Crest Avenue, has 33 campsites, flush toilets, showers, and food lockers. Stone Creek Campground, about 6 miles past Idyllwild on Highway 243, is more remote, with 50 campsites and no showers. Fees vary. 800/444-PARK.

All of the San Jacinto Mountains beyond Mount San Jacinto State Park are part of the vast **San Bernardino National Forest**. There are a number of developed and primitive campgrounds available, along with picnic areas. Drop by the ranger station (54-270 Pine Crest Ave) for maps, regulations, permits (free), and parking passes ($5).

Mountain biking. Mountain bikes are allowed on all dirt roads and most trails in the Idyllwild area, with the exception of the following: the Pacific Crest Trail, interpretive nature trails, and any routes within Designated Wilderness areas. Eti-

Forest fire lookout towers date back to the 1930s in these parts, and some are open to the public during fire season (roughly June through November). Volunteers staff the towers between 9am and 5pm daily. To visit a tower near Idyllwild, take Highway 243 north past town about 8 miles to Black Mountain Road, also known as Forest Road 4S01. Take this dirt road 5.3 miles up through the forest. Make a sharp left turn and drive another 0.5 mile to the end of the road, then follow the paved trail to the tower.

quette requires that mountain bikers yield to hikers and horses and stay on designated trails to help prevent erosion and damage to natural habitats. Obviously, your bike should be in good condition, especially the tires and brakes; rangers recommend bringing both tools and a first aid kit along. A helmet's not a bad idea, either.

See a movie—or rent one. It's easy to spot the Rustic Theatre in the center of town—it's the place with the cheery, sky-blue exterior and the scent of fresh popcorn topped with real butter wafting through the windows. The winsome one-screen movie theater was built in 1952, with seating for 262 and an old-fashioned curtain over the screen. It's a local hangout, both for moviegoers and those who stop by to rent videos from the extensive selection, and it often stays open well after show-time while folks discuss the show and catch up on visiting. Proprietor Marsha Bronson says that in this day of the corporate multiplex, many of the younger visitors have never seen a one-screen theater like this before. And the theater isn't just a draw for locals: some of the more well-known visitors here over the years have included Ted Danson, Michelle Phillips, and Elliott Gould. Movies begin at 7pm each weekday, with three shows on Saturday (at 2, 7, and 9pm) Films are generally current releases, with the occasional art film tossed in to enliven the mix. Adults, $6.50; seniors, $5; kids under 11, $4; all seats $4 on Tuesday nights. (54-290 N Circle Dr near the center of town; 909/659-2747.)

It's just horse sense: The National Forest Service asks that equestrians using local trails pack out all of their trash, avoid grazing horses in meadows, and never bathe horses in lakes and streams.

Horseback riding. The Hay Dude Ranch on the road to Idyllwild has a string of trail horses waiting to take you riding for an hour or even all day. (Hint: If you don't ride regularly, an all-day jaunt may leave you achy for a few days.) The ranch specializes in sunset rides with spectacular views and picnic rides with a break for lunch in the mountains. Rates are $25 an hour (minimum of two riders); special rates available for all-day rides or groups. Open on weekends; midweek reservations need to be made at least 24 hours in advance. The ranch is on McCall Road, just past the McCall Equestrian Park horse camp; 909/763-2473; www.idyllwild.com/haydude.htm.

Jazz festival. Idyllwild's annual Jazz in the Pines brings two days of music to the campus of Idyllwild Arts Academy every summer. Both indoor and outdoor venues provide a showcase for the performers who gather for this pleasantly informal affair, which includes blues and soul as well as jazz. Along with tunes, this fest features an arts and crafts show. Ticket prices vary; kids under 12 can attend for free when accompanied by an adult. No pets; 909/659-3774; info@idyllwildjazz.com; www.idyllwildjazz.com.

Winter sports. Snowfall in Idyllwild varies, but can be up to 60 inches a year. Cross-country skiing draws plenty of participants, and while there are no official ski trails in Idyllwild, you can use closed Forest Trail roads. Inner tubing, sledding, and snowshoeing are also perennial favorites; in the interest of being a good neighbor, watch for private property signs and respect "No

Pick up picnic fix-
ings or the ingredi-
ents for a quick
dinner in your
cabin at one of the
markets in the
heart of downtown
Idyllwild. The Vil-
lage Market
(909/659-3169) car-
ries ready-to-eat
rotisserie chicken,
sandwiches, all
kinds of deli items,
fresh pies, cold
beer, and wine.

Trespassing" notices. In Idyllwild, Nomad Ventures (54-415 N
Circle Dr; 909/659-4853) rents cross-country skis, snowshoes,
sleds, and other winter gear. Open Thursday through Monday.

RESTAURANTS

BREAD BASKET ★★

Folks come to the Bread Basket knowing exactly what
they're going to get: generous helpings of unabashedly
American fare, right down to the chicken-fried steak and
the cranberry sauce served with the roast chicken. The dinner menu here is a step back in time to the days when soup
or salad always came with your meal, and the words "nou-
velle cuisine" were but a glimmer in some baby chef's eyes.
Order the half roast chicken, for example, and a bird the size
of a small turkey arrives on an oversize platter overflowing
with real mashed potatoes (not from a box), freshly steamed
squash, homemade stuffing, and gravy. It's like something
out of a Norman Rockwell painting, and you can see the
delight on the faces of the locals and the tourists, the senior
citizens, the backpackers, the honeymooners, and the
young families with baby strollers. Seating options include
the very pretty front patio—a wooden deck surrounded
with pine trees and blooming shrubs and flowers—or the
cottagelike interior, a series of small, wallpapered rooms
reminiscent of your Midwestern relatives' cabin by the lake.
Breakfast and lunch are also served here, and the place is
rightfully well known for bakery items such as scones and
chocolate eclairs. The selection of tempting microbrews is
much better than the uninspired wine list. Service can be
slow, depending on the number of diners and the number
of servers on duty. *54-710 N Circle Dr, Idyllwild; 909/659-
3506; $; AE, DIS, MC, V; no checks; breakfast, lunch every day;
dinner Fri–Tue; beer and wine only; no reservations; near Fern
Valley.*

GASTROGNOME ★★

Locals and regulars call this place "the Gnome," and it's
cozy enough for any forest creature. Gastrognome combines hearty fare and fine dining to suit mountain appetites

quickened by a day on the trails high above town. Set in the pine forest that swathes most of Idyllwild, the restaurant has a rustic-chic vibe, from the floor-to-ceiling wine rack made of stacked clay pipe to the polished copper panels and wood-paneled walls. Come in on a chilly night, and beneath a spectacular landscape painting you'll find a roaring blaze in the stone fireplace. Dinner features tasty skewered shrimp brushed with mustard sauce and broiled to pink perfection. Other seafood choices include equally simple versions of broiled salmon, halibut, and lobster. Meat eaters choose rack of lamb, or tournedos of beef capped with mushrooms and béarnaise sauce. Lunch takes an informal tack (the Gnome offers one of the better hamburgers in town) and can be eaten on either of two decks outside. *54-381 Ridgeview Dr, Idyllwild; 909/659-5055; $$; AE, DC, DIS, MC, V; no checks; lunch Mon–Sat, dinner every day, brunch Sun; full bar; reservations recommended; www.thegnome.com; turn off Hwy 243 at Texaco and go 1 block.* &

HIDDEN VILLAGE ★★★

Overheard during lunch at this Chinese restaurant in the center of town: "This is so good, I could eat here every day." We'll second that emotion, since the Sichuan and other Chinese cuisine served at this local landmark is outstanding. Situated next door to the Victorian splendor of the Cedar Creek Inn, Hidden Village sports a cheerful red exterior, a pair of golden lions, and a spacious, inviting front patio. Chef/owner Freeman Ye, a native of Beijing, turns out fine renditions of all kinds of traditional dishes, including Kung Pao chicken or shrimp, Peking duck, steamed dumplings, paper-wrapped chicken, and hot 'n' sour soup. Seasonings are bold, ingredients fresh, and service gracious (although not everyone here speaks English as adeptly as Chef Ye). Meals are available à la carte or family style (the latter includes appetizers and soup along with several entrees), and low-priced lunch specials are offered during the week. Have a seat in the comfortably worn dining room under the Chinese lanterns, savor the aromas of ginger and garlic drifting out from the kitchen, and enjoy this slice of Asia here in Idyllwild. *25-840 Cedar St, Idyllwild; 909/659-2712;*

$; MC, V; no checks; lunch, dinner Wed–Mon; beer and wine only; no reservations; corner of N Circle Dr and Cedar St, next door to the Cedar Street Inn.

IDYLLWILD CAFE ★★

They serve breakfast all day at this corner cafe, which is decorated in typically funky Idyllwild style. You know the look: gingham curtains, rough-paneled walls, rustic bric-a-brac (a Western saddle, assorted kitchenware, a set of antlers, an apron reading, "Who Invited All These Tacky People?"), icicle lights hanging from the eaves. But don't let the country-cuteness scare you away: This place delivers when it comes to good service and simple, well-prepared breakfasts. Settle into one of the tables by the windows or out on the patio, where you can smell the pines, and then choose between a handful of three-egg omelets, eggs Benedict, scrambled egg burritos, breakfast steak, or biscuits and gravy. The pleasant waitresses know right when your cup of joe needs topping off. Combo breakfasts featuring French toast, a waffle, or pancakes, along with eggs any style and your choice of bacon or sausage, are an especially good value at around $4.50. (We're especially fond of the French toast, which has a lovely custardy exterior and a subtle cinnamon taste, and the plate-size buckwheat pancakes.) Sure, the place is showing its age, with a faded carpet and scuff marks where satisfied diners have pushed back their chairs into the windowsills for years. But that's part of the charm. *26-600 Hwy 243; 909/659-2210; $; DIS, MC, V; no checks; breakfast, lunch every day (7am–2pm); no alcohol; no reservations; corner of Saunders Meadow Rd and Hwy 243.*

JO'AN'S RESTAURANT & BAR ★★

With a central location in the heart of the village, Jo'An's draws a mix of residents and visitors for breakfast, lunch, dinner, happy hour, Monday night football, Friday night prime rib, and Saturday evening entertainment. This is a down-to-earth, something-for-everyone kind of place with a wide-ranging menu to match. Juicy, cooked-to-order hamburgers with crisp slivers of fries are one of the best reasons to stop in for lunch or dinner, but don't overlook the hot and cold sandwiches, half dozen salads, barbecued baby back ribs, and chicken pot pie. Mexican dishes, pastas, and even a couple of pizzas round out the selection, while Friday and Saturday nights bring a prime rib special followed by live music that often lasts past midnight. The spacious eatery feels like a big log cabin, with a soaring A-frame ceiling, plenty of windows, a choice of tables or booths and a flower-filled patio out back. This is a homey place, where waitresses take the time to chat with patrons, and children are welcomed with a low-priced menu of proven favorites like grilled cheese, chicken tenders, French toast, and cinnamon toast. For dessert, there's Mud Pie or hot fudge sundaes—guaranteed to please the 10-year-old in all of us. *25-070 Village Center Dr, Idyllwild; 909/659-0295; $; AE, DIS, MC, V; local checks only; breakfast, lunch, dinner every day; full bar; no reservations; on Village Center Dr across from the Fort.*

LODGINGS

CEDAR STREET INN   ★★

Here's a getaway spot that offers old-fashioned Victorian charm with all the modern conveniences. The main house and gazebo out front are pleasingly formal and as pretty as a wedding cake (indeed, several weddings have been held here in the gardens), and form the entryway to a series of cozy cottages and suites. The rooms, decorated with collectibles and antiques from the owners' collection, are romantic without being fussy, and each follows a different theme. The handsome Captain's Quarters has a rock fireplace, brass bed, wood paneling, and a real claw-footed tub, while the unique Attic Room requires a spiral staircase to reach the sleeping quarters and private deck. All rooms include a fireplace and private bath. Freestanding cabins include a tidy little cottage, perfect for two; a couple of two-story cabins that can accommodate four guests; and a sweet two-bedroom cabin with deck and Jacuzzi. Quiet time is encouraged here; the communal parlor offers a selection of books, puzzles, and games, and each room includes a coffeemaker so you needn't venture into town for your morning caffeine fix. Smoking and pets are prohibited. *25-880 Cedar St, Idyllwild; 909/659-4789; $$; MC, V; checks OK; www.cedarstreetinn.com; off N Circle Dr on Cedar St just past Hidden Village restaurant.*

CEDAR VIEW COTTAGE ★★

Definitely one-of-a-kind, this historic cottage behind a ceramic-artist's studio dates to the 1920s, when it was owned by a screenwriter. The current owner, artist Grace Songolo, has updated it to include a fully equipped kitchen (complete with espresso machine and coffee grinder), entertainment center (TV, VCR, stereo with lots of CDs), and gas barbecue, but the quirky and original charm remains. Downstairs there's a master bedroom decorated with dozens of framed mirrors, a full bath, and a living room with a wood-burning fireplace. Climb the steep, narrow staircase to the loft, and you'll find two twin beds and a small bath. Fresh flowers and chocolates on your pillow each night add a dash of elegance to the rustic ambience. The cottage, surrounded by trees, is close to the center of town and within walking distance of assorted shops, restaurants, and the movie theater. Well-behaved dogs are welcome (for a small extra charge); a doggie-door opens to a small, fenced outdoor run. *25-165 Cedar St, Idyllwild; 909/659-3339 (information) or 909/659-2966 (reservations); $$; MC, V; no checks; www.towncrier.com/inns/cedarview.html; just off N Circle Dr on Cedar St behind the Songolo Gallery.*

CREEKSTONE INN ★★

 Stepping into this elegant two-story bed-and-breakfast—originally constructed in the early 1940s—is like walking into a welcoming family home. Decorated with antiques, seasonal wreaths, wood paneling, and fresh flowers, the inn's main sitting room radiates charm and warmth. One side is dominated by a big stone fireplace; across the room, there's a small bar for morning coffee or an evening glass of wine. Breakfast is included in the price and is served in a cheery sunroom off to one side. Just nine guest rooms are available (all with queen-size bed and private bath), on either the first or second floor. Quaint country-style furnishings give each room a decidedly old-fashioned look, so it's a bit of a surprise to see the modern double Jacuzzi tubs available in three of the suites. One even has a dramatic, double-sided fireplace that opens into the bathroom as well as the bedroom. Situated at Fern Valley Corners on the upper end of town, the Creekstone Inn offers gracious living and some splendid mountain views, and it's within walking distance of several shops. *54-950 Pine Crest Ave, Idyllwild; 909/659-3342 or 800/409-2127; $$; AE, MC, V; checks OK; www.idyl.com; at the corner of Pine Crest Ave and N Circle Dr.*

IDYLLWILD INN ★

Idyllwild Inn, family-owned since 1909, scatters its 15 cabins through an open pine forest like a gracious little Tyrolean village. Families love it here, and although the inn doesn't have a pool, the tots' playground is a good substitute. Cabins are neat, with a simple mountain decor; each has a wood-burning fireplace, kitchen, and deck. Some were built as early as 1909, others in the 1930s, and the newest—the duplexes—in the 1980s, although it's obvious all have been constantly maintained and upgraded. The bustle of Idyllwild is literally outside the front gate, but once inside this compound you really feel you're in a mountain town. At some point asphalt drives were put in so you could drive right to your cabin, and unfortunately they tend to dominate the setting a bit; when you reserve, ask to be on the side farthest from the entrance. *54-300 Village Center Dr, Idyllwild; 888/659-2552; $–$$; DIS, MC, V; checks OK; www.idyll wildinn.com; from Hwy 243, turn onto Ridgeview Rd at the Texaco station and go 2 blocks to Village Center.* &

QUIET CREEK INN ★★★

Few inns are better named than this classy property a short drive from the center of town. Located at a quiet corner just above Strawberry Creek, the inn is one of the newest hotels in town, with five stylish cabin duplexes a short distance from the owners' home. Each cabin offers both a studio and a one-bedroom suite, equipped with wood-burning fireplace, fully stocked kitchenette, cable TV, and a private balcony overlooking the forest and creek. Accommodations are immaculate and well tended, with designer touches like Berber carpeting and cathedral ceilings. A large barn on the property has been transformed into a family room of sorts, where guests can use the microwave oven, make phone calls (there are no phones in the guest quarters), assemble puzzles, flip through local restaurant menus, or simply hang out. Blue jays, nuthatches, robins, and woodpeckers are a few of the birds attracted by water bowls and feeders, and bold, twitchy-tailed gray squirrels are as common as pinecones. The place has a contemplative, peaceful aura that makes it a fine place for adults who want to unwind over a good novel by the fire, on the deck, or at one of the chairs thoughtfully placed alongside the stream. Note: The owners of Quiet Creek also handle bookings for a two-bedroom log cabin with full kitchen across the street from the inn. *26-345 Delano Dr, Idyllwild; 909/659-6110 or 800/450-6110; $; MC, V; checks OK; qci@pe.net; www.quietcreekinn.com; from Hwy 243 take Tollgate Rd to Delano Dr and turn right.*

STRAWBERRY CREEK INN ★★

One of the first bed-and-breakfasts in the region and long one of the best, Strawberry Creek has a location just far enough outside town (about a quarter mile) to grant it the peace and quiet mountain visitors seek. Yes, there is a Strawberry Creek, and a walking path leads along it all the way into town. The inn was fashioned by owners Diana Dugan and Jim Goff from a large, shingled cabin that was built in 1941. Five rooms in the main cabin put you closest to the large living room/recreation room/library downstairs—the true heart of the house and a great place to gather around a fire on chilly days. Four rooms out back on the "courtyard" are newer but feel a bit less cozy, and there's a small single cabin close to the creek. Decor elements include a range of window seats, antique bed frames, wood-burning fireplaces, and skylights; all rooms have private baths. A full breakfast is served out on a big glassed-in porch. Smoking is prohibited. *26-370 Hwy 243, Idyllwild; 909/659-3202 or 800/262-8969; $–$$; DIS, MC, V; checks OK; www.strawberrycreekinn.com; 0.5 mile south of the village.* &

WOODLAND PARK MANOR ★★★

The spacious, sloping grounds of this property are home to several modern duplex cottages, each with its own deck. Their simple but dramatic design, with open-beam ceilings and floor-to-ceiling windows, creates a bright, open feeling inside, not to mention front-row seats on nature's continuous floor show. Birds, squirrels, and the occasional raccoon provide the outdoor entertainment; indoors, each unit has cable TV and a VCR. The larger side of each cabin has a completely equipped kitchen, fireplace, and both a queen and a double bed. The other half offers a queen bed and fireplace, and while there's no kitchen, a refrigerator and coffeemaker are included. All accommodations are simply furnished with wood furniture, cheery bedspreads, and light-colored paneled walls. This is a popular spot for families during the summer, when the heated pool (a fairly rare commodity in these parts) is open. There's also a Ping-Pong table and picnic area. In addition to the duplex cabins, Woodland Park Manor rents out a freestanding cottage in the woods, with kitchen, barbecue, queen-size bed, fireplace, and a hammock. *55-350 S Circle Dr, Idyllwild; 909/659-2657; $; MC, V; checks OK; www.woodlandparkmanor.com; off S Circle Dr near Fern Valley Rd.*

GOLF

GOLF

Truly a golfer's Promised Land, the Palm Springs region features close to 100 courses, ranging from easy nine-hole beginners' links to brilliantly wicked tournament courses that can bring a pro to tears.

Nowhere on earth do so many golf courses cluster in such close proximity as in California's low desert. Nor is there any finer weather for playing what Mark Twain called "a good walk spoiled": the area averages 350 sunny days a year.

The improbability of the setting may well be its main attraction: lush fairways nestling amidst sun-scorched sand and rock, while a stern curtain of mountains rises like a silent playing partner watching your every drive. The experience can be intensely artificial yet satisfying at the same time.

Serious golfers don't care much about analyzing their addiction, however. They want answers: Who designed the course? What is its slope rating and reputation among players? What pro tournaments has it hosted? When can I get on? And how much will a round cost?

In Palm Springs and other nearby resort cities, that last element can add up fast. Most greens fees run in the $100-and-up range during the cooler winter and spring seasons. Fees over $200 per round are not unheard of. At the same time, you can still get on numerous public courses for $50 or less. And those willing to play in summer can enjoy tremendous discounts (see "Beat the Heat" for details).

One special challenge: It's not easy to tell which courses are public, semiprivate, or private. A course's name tells you little about its exclusivity or openness. Many "clubs" are open to the public and are essentially public courses. Resorts often have their own courses, and guests and members have priority.

To sort out some of the mystery, visiting golfers often either turn to their hotel concierge (most concierges have "ins" with various nearby courses for tee times) or contact booking agencies directly.

For a list of current, reliable agencies, contact the Palm Springs Visitors Information Center (760/778-8418 or 800/347-7746; www.palm-springs.org) or the Palm Springs Desert Resorts Convention and Visitors' Bureau (800/96-RESORTS; www.desert-resorts.com). From the latter, you can also order a

THE GRASS IS GREENER, PART 1

Lusting after those oh-so-manicured greens and rarefied air of a private club? With exclusive membership policies and initiations that can be over $50,000, private golf courses are out of reach for the majority of players. But you've got a chance, even if you lack a well-heeled member/friend to invite you to play as a guest. Several private clubs sell their unused tee times through brokering services, usually after 4pm on the day before play. Fewer tee times are generally available during the summer, when many private courses replace greens or rework irrigation. But you can still use these last-minute reservation services to save a bundle at public and semiprivate courses, which often offer next-day play for a discount of at least 50 percent. Check the Palm Springs Desert Resorts Convention and Visitors' Bureau for a list of recommended services; 800/96-RESORTS; www.desert-resorts.com.

brochure ($2.95) that lists every single golf course in the area, along with phone number, address, course designer, and the like.

The visitors' bureaus also offer information on "passbooks" offering multiple-course discounts, PGA tournament schedules (if you enjoy being a spectator), and even golf guides who speak Japanese, German, or other languages.

For anyone with Internet access, the bureaus' Web sites offer a number of links to individual course information (including course layouts). Or, log on to your favorite golf magazine's site. Another invaluable source of information is *The Desert Sun* newspaper's on-line edition (www.thedesertsun.com), which includes detailed reviews and photos of many local courses by golf writer Larry Bohannon.

Bohannon, who's played about 68 of the courses in the region and has toured at least 28 more, singled out the following seven as some of his favorites.

All greens fees listed are approximate, and refer to premium winter rates during the week. Prices can vary on weekends.

PRIVATE GOLF COURSES

Golfers' dress code: a collared shirt and tailored shorts (or slacks); no T-shirts or cutoffs. An increasing number of courses are requiring soft-spiked shoes to reduce damage to greens, so be prepared.

WESTIN MISSION HILLS, RANCHO MIRAGE

Like many resorts in the valley, the Westin offers two separate courses. Both offer practice facilities and equipment rental. The Resort Course, a par 70 by notorious designer Pete Dye, is the more difficult, with deep bunkers, elevated tees, and plenty of chances to get into trouble. The Signature Course offers a good test as well, however, and is popular for its lush landscaping, rolling fairways, and numerous lakes. *760/328-3198; fee per course: $150; Resort Course: 71-501 Dinah Shore Dr. From Palm Springs, take Ramon Rd to Bob Hope Dr, go south to Dinah Shore Dr, then turn right. Signature Course: 70-705 Ramon Rd. Take I-10 to Ramon Rd, then go east on Ramon Rd for about 4 miles.*

PGA WEST, LA QUINTA

This semiprivate resort is home to one of the most famous (or infamous) courses in the country—the tough TPC Stadium Course, designed by Pete Dye. A par 72, it's a challenge even for the pros, with gigantic bunkers, tricky greens, and oceans of water. Bohannon jokingly describes it as "more like an amusement park than a golf course." Mid-level players can probably get around here, but expect three-digit scores and a lot of lost balls, and avoid the pro-level black tees.

The Jack Nicklaus Tournament Course is also a toughie, though not quite as harrowing as playing the Stadium. This par 72, designed by Nicklaus himself, has lots of lakes and enough bunkers to make errant players think they're in the Sahara. *760/564-7170; www.pgawest.com; fee per course: approx. $225–$235; 56-150 PGA Blvd, La Quinta. Head east on I-10 to the Indio Boulevard exit, then follow Jefferson St south about 5 miles to the resort on the left.*

LANDMARK GOLF CLUB, INDIO

Pete Dye designed both of the impressive new courses at Landmark, which hosted the popular Skins game in 1999 and will continue to do so for the next several years. For the Skins tournament, the North and South Courses are combined (nine holes played on each). Both courses are challenging par 72s and are beautifully woven into the desert landscape, with gorgeous views and rolling hills. *760/775-2000; www.landmarkgc.com; fee per course: $125; 84-000 Landmark Pkwy, Indio. Take I-10 east to Golf Center Parkway exit, go north 1.5 miles to Landmark Pkwy, entrance on right.*

TAHQUITZ CREEK GOLF RESORT, PALM SPRINGS

Although this public facility sees a lot of action, it's well maintained and stays in remarkably good condition. Choose between the new Resort Course, designed by Ted Robinson, Jr., with his signature bounty of water hazards, and the popular Legends Course, a flatter layout with no water but many a bunker. Grass tee driving range; equipment rental. *760/328-1005 or 800/743-2211; www.tahquitz creek.com; fee per course: Legends, $60; Resort, $80; 1885 Golf Club Dr, Palm Springs. Take Ramon Rd east to Crossley Rd to entrance.*

LA QUINTA RESORT AND CLUB, LA QUINTA

Two wicked Pete Dye courses attract players in search of a good test to this legendary resort. The Dunes Course, Dye's very first project in the desert area, features looming sand traps and plenty of water. And the Mountain Course—consistently voted one of the top places to play in the country—sports the famous 16th hole: "A tee and a green, with nothing but rocks in between." Work out the kinks after a round here at the luxurious spa—reason to visit even if you're not a golf aficionado. *760/564-7610; www.laquinta resort.com; fee per course: Dunes, $145; Mountain, $225; 50-200 Avenue Vista Bonita, La Quinta. Take I-10 or Hwy 111 to Washington St, go south to 50th Ave, then west across Eisenhower Dr.*

MARRIOTT DESERT SPRINGS, PALM DESERT

Ted Robinson, Sr., created the two beautiful courses here, using abundant water and bunkers to add drama to the wide fairways. This resort appeals to players of all levels. Folks who only play a few times a year will find both the

BEAT THE HEAT

Summer's three-digit temperatures can mean unbelievable deals for the intrepid golfer. A course that charges $160 per round during the peak winter season might go for $40 in July or August. Too, a number of top-notch resorts sell generous package deals, offering a room, unlimited golf, and often a free dinner or spa treatment for less than the regular price of a room. For example: Rooms at the delectable Miramonte in Indian Wells start at around $200 during high season. But in July, they were selling one of their spacious suites plus golf at several nearby courses for $89 per night.

The key to playing when it's 105°F by noon? Play as early as you can (most courses open by 6am); bring lots of water, and drink plenty during the game; consider wearing a wet towel, dampened periodically with ice water, around your neck; wear a hat; and slather on the sunscreen throughout the day. And don't expect the usual amenities during the summer. Golfer Bill Fairbanks, who visits the desert for a golf trip with his buddies every summer, found some of the snack bars closed, both at the first tee and the ninth hole turn, which meant no place to buy water or other refreshments.

"If you're going to play good golf, you really have to plan ahead," said Fairbanks, who managed to get in 36 holes on a 107°F day. "Every nine holes, I try to drink two big Gatorades." He also recommends hitting the course by 7am for a morning round, then returning around 4:30 or 5 to play again. "Of course, by the 18th hole, we couldn't see the ball!"

Finally, know the signs of heat stroke if you're playing during the summer. Nausea, dizziness, goosebumps, and vision difficulties are all reasons to stop playing, get into the shade, and get rehydrated.

Palms and the Valley Courses challenging, but relatively forgiving, while experts can use the black tees to add distance and difficulty. *760/341-1756; fee per course: approx. $160; 74-855 Country Club Dr, Palm Desert. Take Ramon Rd to Bob Hope Dr and go south to Country Club Dr, then east.*

"The reason the pro
tells you to keep
your head down is
so you can't see
him laughing."
—Phyllis Diller

DESERT WILLOW GOLF RESORT, PALM DESERT

These newer, "environmentally sensitive" courses feature a lot less turf and a lot more desert sand than conventional links. The Firecliff Course includes a plethora of bunkers and some serious desert rough; Bohannon says, "If you can't keep it straight, don't play here." Slightly less intimidating is the Mountain View Course. Both of these imaginative designs offer striking views and brilliant use of the natural desert landscape. *760/346-7060; www.desertwillow.com; fee per course: $130; 38-955 Desert Willow Dr, Palm Desert. Take I-10 east to Cook St, then south to Country Club Dr and west to entrance (across from Marriott Desert Springs Resort).*

PUBLIC GOLF COURSES

Below, we've included a selection of some of the popular public courses throughout the valley.

Cathedral Canyon Country Club (34-567 Cathedral Canyon Dr, Cathedral City; 760/328-6571) offers three 9-hole courses, two of them with lots of water, and a driving range.

Cimarron (67-603 30th Ave, Cathedral City; 760/770-6060), with two 18-hole courses known simply as the Long Course and the Short Course, is one of the newest resorts in the desert.

Date Palm Country Club (36-200 Date Palm Dr, Cathedral City; 760/328-1315) features 18 holes; designed by Ted Robinson, Sr., it is slightly hilly and heavy on traps.

Desert Dunes Golf Course (19-300 Palm Dr, Desert Hot Springs; 760/251-5366), designed by Robert Trent Jones Jr., has 18 holes and was the site of the 1999 Senior PGA Tour Qualifier.

Desert Falls Country Club (1111 Desert Falls Parkway, Palm Desert; 760/340-5646) offers 18 holes; it's mildly hilly with abundant bunkers.

Golf Center at Palm Desert (74-945 Sheryl Dr, Palm Desert; 760/779-1877) is an 18-hole executive course with a lighted driving range.

Heritage Palms Golf Club (44-291 Heritage Palms Dr S, Indio; 760/772-7334), with 18 holes, is an open, gently rolling course designed by Arthur Hill.

Indian Springs Golf Course (46-080 Jefferson St, La Quinta; 760/775-3360) has an 18-hole design that is undergoing an extensive renovation; players are looking forward to a new, improved course.

Indian Wells Golf Resort (44-500 Indian Wells Lane, Indian Wells; 760/346-4653) has North and South Courses; both are 18-hole Ted Robinson, Sr., designs with a number of lakes.

Indio Municipal Golf Club (83-040 Avenue 42, Indio; 760/347-9156) is an 18-hole executive course; no advance tee time required.

Mesquite Country Club (2700 East Mesquite Ave, Palm Springs; 760/323-9377) features 18 holes and is known as one of the best-maintained public courses in the area.

Mission Lakes Country Club (8484 Clubhouse Blvd, Desert Hot Springs; 760/329-8061) has 18 holes; it's designed by Ted Robinson, Sr.

Palm Desert Resort Country Club (77-333 Country Club Dr, Palm Desert; 760/345-2791) offers 18 holes and is known for its challenging, unusual design.

Oasis Country Club (42-300 Casbah Way, Palm Desert; 760/345-2715) has 18 holes, with lots of water and traps; no cart required.

> *"There is an old saying: 'If a man comes home with sand in his cuffs and cockleburrs in his pants, don't ask him what he shot.'"*
> —Sam Snead

THE GRASS IS GREENER, PART 2

How do they keep these courses looking so fabulous? Part of the secret is overseeding, a process that keeps the turf on the desert golf courses as green as a Masters jacket all year round. During fall and winter, the Bermuda grass used on courses tends to go dormant, and turns an unappealing yellow-brown. The groundskeepers "overseed" by sowing rye grass, an annual, to green up courses until the following spring. Why should you care? Because many courses close down for several weeks, any time from late September into early November to complete the transition, and it can be difficult to find a place to play. Call ahead during these times of year to make sure the course of your choice is operating.

INDEX

BEST PLACES
DESTINATIONS
PALM SPRINGS
REPORT FORM

Based on my personal experience, I wish to nominate the following restaurant or place of lodging; or confirm/correct/disagree with the current review.

_____

_____

_____

_____

(Please include address and telephone number of establishment, if convenient.)

REPORT

Please describe food, service, style, comfort, value, date of visit, and other aspects of your experience; continue on another piece of paper if necessary.

_____

_____

_____

_____

_____

_____

I am not concerned, directly or indirectly, with the management or ownership of this establishment.

SIGNED _____

ADDRESS _____

_____

PHONE _____ **DATE** _____

Please address to Best Places Destinations and send to:

SASQUATCH BOOKS
615 Second Avenue, Suite 260
Seattle, WA 98104
Feel free to email feedback as well: books@sasquatchbooks.com

BEST PLACES
DESTINATIONS
PALM SPRINGS
REPORT FORM

Based on my personal experience, I wish to nominate the following restaurant or place of lodging; or confirm/correct/disagree with the current review.

_____

_____

_____

_____

(Please include address and telephone number of establishment, if convenient.)

REPORT

Please describe food, service, style, comfort, value, date of visit, and other aspects of your experience; continue on another piece of paper if necessary.

_____

_____

_____

_____

_____

_____

_____

I am not concerned, directly or indirectly, with the management or ownership of this establishment.

SIGNED _____

ADDRESS _____

_____

_____

PHONE _____ DATE _____

Please address to Best Places Destinations and send to:

SASQUATCH BOOKS
615 Second Avenue, Suite 260
Seattle, WA 98104
Feel free to email feedback as well: books@sasquatchbooks.com

TRUST THE LOCALS
BEST PLACES®

REGIONAL GUIDES

**Best Places
Southern California**
$19.95

**Best Places
Northwest**
$19.95

**Best Places
Northern California**
$19.95

**Best Places
Alaska**
$21.95

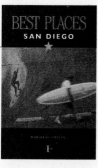

CITY GUIDES

**Best Places
San Diego**
$18.95

**Best Places
Las Vegas**
$18.95

**Best Places
San Francisco**
$18.95

**Best Places
Seattle**
$18.95

**Best Places
Los Angeles**
$18.95

**Best Places
Phoenix**
$18.95

**Best Places
Portland**
$18.95

**Best Places
Vancouver**
$18.95

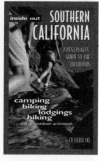

ADVENTURE TRAVEL

**Inside Out
Southern
California**
$21.95

**Inside Out
Oregon**
$21.95

**Inside Out
British Columbia**
$21.95

**Inside Out
Northern
California**
$21.95

**Inside Out
Washington**
$21.95

**Inside Out
Northern Rockies**
$21.95

DESTINATIONS

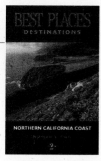

**Northern
California Coast**
$12.95

**San Juan
& Gulf Islands**
$12.95

Oregon Coast
$11.95

**California's
Wine Country**
$12.95

**Olympic
Peninsula**
$12.95

Palm Springs
$14.95